| Hate Groups

Other Books in the Current Controversies Series

| Hate Groups

Adam Furgang and
Erica Grove, Book Editors

GREENHAVEN
PUBLISHING

Published in 2022 by Greenhaven Publishing, LLC
353 3rd Avenue, Suite 255, New York, NY 10010

Articles in Greenhaven Publishing anthologies are often edited for length to meet page
requirements. In addition, original titles of these works are changed to clearly present
the main thesis and to explicitly indicate the author's opinion. Every effort is made to
ensure that Greenhaven Publishing accurately reflects the original intent of the authors.
Every effort has been made to trace the owners of the copyrighted material.

Cover image: John Bazemore/AP Images.

Library of Congress Cataloging-in-Publication Data

Names: Furgang, Adam, editor.
Title: Hate groups / Adam Furgang and Erica Grove, book editors.
Description: First edition. | New York, NY : Greenhaven Publishing, 2022. |
Series: Current controversies | Includes bibliographical references and
index. | Contents: Hate groups | Audience: Ages 15+ | Audience: Grades
10–12 | Summary: "Anthology of diverse perspectives in point-counterpoint format,
with volume introduction and resource materials."— Provided by publisher.
Identifiers: LCCN 2020049125 | ISBN 9781534507784 (library binding) | ISBN
  9781534507760 (paperback) | ISBN 9781534507791 (ebook)
Subjects: LCSH: Hate crimes—United States—Juvenile literature. | Hate
  groups—United States—Juvenile literature. | Racism—United
  States—Juvenile literature.
Classification: LCC HV6773.52 .H368 2022 | DDC 305.5/68—dc23
LC record available at https://lccn.loc.gov/2020049125

Manufactured in the United States of America

Website: http://greenhavenpublishing.com

Chapter 2: Is It Useful to Label and Monitor Hate Groups?

Chapter 4: Should Hate Groups and Hate Speech Be Illegal?

Yes: Hate Groups and Hate Speech Should Be Prevented and Punished

No: Laws That Make Hate Groups and Hate Speech Illegal Violate First Amendment Rights and Harm Democracy

Foreword

"Controversy" is a word that has an undeniably unpleasant connotation. It carries a definite negative charge. Controversy can spoil family gatherings, spread a chill around classroom and campus discussion, inflame public discourse, open raw civic wounds, and lead to the ouster of public officials. We often feel that controversy is almost akin to bad manners, a rude and shocking eruption of that which must not be spoken or thought of in polite, tightly guarded society. To avoid controversy, to quell controversy, is often seen as a public good, a victory for etiquette, perhaps even a moral or ethical imperative.

Yet the studious, deliberate avoidance of controversy is also a whitewashing, a denial, a death threat to democracy. It is a false sterilizing and sanitizing and superficial ordering of the messy, ragged, chaotic, at times ugly processes by which a healthy democracy identifies and confronts challenges, engages in passionate debate about appropriate approaches and solutions, and arrives at something like a consensus and a broadly accepted and supported way forward. Controversy is the megaphone, the speaker's corner, the public square through which the citizenry finds and uses its voice. Controversy is the life's blood of our democracy and absolutely essential to the vibrant health of our society.

Our present age is certainly no stranger to controversy. We are consumed by fierce debates about technology, privacy, political correctness, poverty, violence, crime and policing, guns, immigration, civil and human rights, terrorism, militarism, environmental protection, and gender and racial equality. Loudly competing voices are raised every day, shouting opposing opinions, putting forth competing agendas, and summoning starkly different visions of a utopian or dystopian future. Often these voices attempt to shout the others down; there is precious little listening and considering among the cacophonous din. Yet listening and considering, too, are essential to the health of a democracy. If controversy is democracy's lusty lifeblood, respectful listening and careful thought are its higher faculties, its brain, its conscience.

Current Controversies does not shy away from or attempt to hush the loudly competing voices. It seeks to provide readers with as wide and representative as possible a range of articulate voices on any given controversy of the day, separates each one out to allow it to be heard clearly and fairly, and encourages careful listening to each of these well-crafted, thoughtfully expressed opinions, supplied by some of today's leading academics, thinkers, analysts, politicians, policy makers, economists, activists, change agents, and advocates. Only after listening to a wide range of opinions on an issue, evaluating the strengths and weaknesses of each argument, assessing how well the facts and available evidence mesh with the stated opinions and conclusions, and thoughtfully and critically examining one's own beliefs and conscience can the reader begin to arrive at his or her own conclusions and articulate his or her own stance on the spotlighted controversy.

This process is facilitated and supported in each Current Controversies volume by an introduction and chapter overviews that provide readers with the essential context they need to begin engaging with the spotlighted controversies, with the debates surrounding them, and with their own perhaps shifting or nascent opinions on them. Chapters are organized around several key questions that are answered with diverse opinions representing all points on the political spectrum. In its content, organization, and methodology, readers are encouraged to determine the authors' point of view and purpose, interrogate and analyze the various arguments and their rhetoric and structure, evaluate the arguments' strengths and weaknesses, test their claims against available facts and evidence, judge the validity of the reasoning, and bring into clearer, sharper focus the reader's own beliefs and conclusions and how they may differ from or align with those in the collection or those of classmates.

Research has shown that reading comprehension skills improve dramatically when students are provided with compelling, intriguing, and relevant "discussable" texts. The subject matter of these collections could not be more compelling, intriguing, or urgently relevant to today's students and the world they are poised to inherit. The anthologized articles also provide the basis for stimulating, lively, and passionate classroom debates. Students who are compelled to anticipate objections to their own argument and identify the flaws in those of an opponent read more carefully, think more critically, and steep themselves in relevant context, facts, and information more thoroughly. In short, using discussable text of the kind provided by every single volume in the Current Controversies series encourages close reading, facilitates reading comprehension, fosters research, strengthens critical thinking, and greatly enlivens and energizes classroom discussion and participation. The entire learning process is deepened, extended, and strengthened.

If we are to foster a knowledgeable, responsible, active, and engaged citizenry, we must provide readers with the intellectual, interpretive, and critical-thinking tools and experience necessary to make sense of the world around them and of the all-important debates and arguments that inform it. We must encourage them not to run away from or attempt to quell controversy but to embrace it in a responsible, conscientious, and thoughtful way, to sharpen and strengthen their own informed opinions by listening to and critically analyzing those of others. This series encourages respectful engagement with and analysis of current controversies and competing opinions and fosters a resulting increase in the strength and rigor of one's own opinions and stances. As such, it helps readers assume their rightful place in the public square and provides them with the skills necessary to uphold their awesome responsibility—guaranteeing the continued and future health of a vital, vibrant, and free democracy.

Introduction

> *"Eastward and westward storms are
> breaking,—great, ugly whirlwinds of
> hatred and blood and cruelty. I will
> not believe them inevitable."*
>
> —W. E. B. Du Bois

According to the Southern Poverty Law Center (SPLC), a hate group is "an organization that—based on its official statements or principles, the statements of its leaders, or its activities—has beliefs or practices that attack or malign an entire class of people, typically for their immutable characteristics."[1] White supremacist groups like the Ku Klux Klan and neo-Nazi organizations frequently come to mind when considering hate groups—which, based on the SPLC's report that there has been a 55 percent increase in white supremacist groups since 2017, is a reasonable assumption to make.[2]

However, hate groups enact all manner of bigoted beliefs and actions. Some groups, like the Nation of Islam and the New Black Panther Party, are considered hate groups for expressing and acting on anti-white sentiments. The fundamentalist Christian group the Family Research Council is considered an anti-LGBTQ+ hate group for dehumanizing and demonizing members of this population.[3]

In many cases, however, it is not so easy to determine whether a group is a hate group. Often when one hate-monitoring organization makes this distinction, other organizations and individuals contest it. For example, in his criticism of the aforementioned Southern Poverty Law Center, Robby Soave takes the center to task for including individuals and small groups of people in its list of hate groups, despite the fact that they lack the membership, organization, or influence to even classify as groups.[4] He also points out that its classification of extremists can be controversial, as is the case with its labeling of British activist Maajid Nawaz as an anti-Muslim extremist, despite his self-professed goal being to de-radicalize Muslim extremists.[5] Though it can be useful to keep track of existing hate groups in an effort to prevent tragic hate crimes from happening—as demonstrated by the fact that the civil rights division of the US Federal Bureau of Investigation (FBI) extensively investigates hundreds of hate groups and hate crimes every year—it is important to critically consider whether these labels are deserved.

Furthermore, there are numerous factors that make it difficult to determine whether hate groups can be held responsible for violent hate crimes. Generally speaking, it is quite easy to tell when a hate crime has been committed, but often it's not so easy to pin the blame on a hate group. For instance, in the case of the 2019 mass shooting at a Walmart parking lot in El Paso, Texas, it is clear that the perpetrator, Patrick Crusius, committed the crime out of hate for a specific group of people, since he posted an anti-Latino manifesto online shortly before the attack and targeted Latinos during his rampage.[6] However, despite his white supremacist beliefs, the attack cannot be attributed to a particular hate group since Crusius acted on his own and was not a known member of any hate groups. One can assert that allowing white supremacist hate groups to exist and have a platform on the internet and in the media emboldens individuals like Crusius to act, but it was difficult to draw a direct connection between these groups and Crusius.

Additionally, just because a political group engages in violent actions does not automatically make it a hate group. Whether or not the far-right group the Proud Boys is a hate group is a major point of contention, a question that was even raised before President Trump during a presidential debate in September 2020.[7] The group has been involved in numerous violent altercations and demonstrations and is accused of misogynistic and white supremacist rhetoric, but the group's official stance includes "longstanding regulations prohibiting racist, white supremacist or violent activity."[8] Because its publicly stated mission is not bigoted in nature, many people do not consider the Proud Boys a hate group. Ultimately, one must decide what matters more: the public mission and beliefs proclaimed by an organization, or the potentially hateful actions it takes and rhetoric it uses.

On the other side of the political spectrum, the far-left group Antifa—short for anti-fascist—raises similar questions. Antifa includes largely decentralized and otherwise unorganized groups of far-left activists who act by confronting those they perceive to be white supremacists or far-right extremists.[9] Due to the militant and confrontational nature of those involved in Antifa—as well as the fact that these violent actions are targeted at individuals and groups based on their political affiliation—some have deemed the group a hate group or a domestic terrorist organization, including President Trump.[10] However, aside from opposing the far-right, there is little that defines or unites the group, so despite the fact that Antifa raises concerns for law enforcement due to some extremist and violent actions, it is difficult to characterize the group as a hate group.

Ultimately, one of the major tensions in the debate surrounding hate groups as well as hate speech is striking a balance between public safety and the freedom of expression. The First Amendment guarantees the freedom of expression through speech and assembly. This means that, even if the things someone says or a group's reason for assembling and demonstrating is controversial or objectionable, people have a constitutional right to express themselves as they wish. However, one's First Amendment rights can be challenged if their expression can present a danger to others, such as by inciting violence. For this reason, some argue that hate speech and the hate groups that spew it should not be protected by the Constitution, causing them to be kicked off online platforms and social media websites and sometimes even arrested. However, others argue that this kind of censorship creates a dangerous precedent and that hate groups and hate speech are too difficult to concretely define. Additionally, some have pointed out that kicking hate groups off platforms and websites has little effect in deterring them, as they often find new ways to assemble and disseminate hate.

The authors of the viewpoints in *Current Controversies: Hate Groups* examine the issue of hate from an array of angles. They present differing perspectives on how hate groups are defined, what can be done to stop hate and its expression, and how to balance personal freedoms with the potential danger presented by hate groups. Though it is undeniably a fraught and complex issue, readers will be empowered to engage in the timely debate surrounding hate groups.

Notes

1. "Frequently Asked Questions About Hate Groups," Southern Poverty Law Center, March 18, 2020, https://www.splcenter.org/20200318/frequently-asked-questions -about-hate-groups#hate%20group.

2. "Executive Summary: 2019 Year in Hate," Southern Poverty Law Center, March 18, 2020, https://www.splcenter.org/news/2020/03/18/executive-summary-2019 -year-hate.

3. "Frequently Asked Questions About Hate Groups," Southern Poverty Law Center, March 18, 2020, https://www.splcenter.org/20200318/frequently-asked-questions -about-hate-groups.

4. Robby Soave, "The Southern Poverty Law Center Is Both a Terrible Place to Work and a Place That Does Terrible Work," *Reason*, March 27, 2019, https://reason .com/2019/03/27/southern-poverty-law-center-hate-crime/.

5. Ibid.

6. Andrew Blankenstein and Minyvonne Burke, "El Paso Shooting: 20 People Dead, 26 Injured, Suspect in Custody, Police Say," *NBC News*, August 3, 2019, https:// www.nbcnews.com/news/us-news/active-shooter-near-el-paso-mall-police -responding-n1039001.

7. "Who Are the Proud Boys and Antifa and Are They Terrorists?" the *Week,* September 30, 2020, https://www.theweek.co.uk/107137/what-is-antifa-are-they -terrorists.

8. Joel Shannon, "Who Are the Proud Boys? Far-Right Group Has Concerned Experts for Years," *USA Today*, September 30, 2020, https://www.usatoday.com /story/news/nation/2020/09/30/who-proud-boys-group-mentioned-debate-has -violent-history/5868406002/.

9. "Who Are Antifa?" ADL, https://www.adl.org/resources/backgrounders/who-are -antifa.

10. "Who Are the Proud Boys and Antifa and Are They Terrorists?" the *Week,* September 30, 2020, https://www.theweek.co.uk/107137/what-is-antifa-are-they -terrorists.

| Is Hate Learned?

Overview: Hate Crimes Are Common in the United States

Cas Mudde

Cas Mudde is a columnist for the US edition of the Guardian *and a professor in the School of Public and International Affairs at the University of Georgia.*

D o the names Elijah Coverdale, Kathy Finley or Tywanza Sanders sound familiar? Probably not. And yet you are almost certain to know the names of the men who killed them. Elijah Coverdale and Kathy Finley were two of the 168 people killed in the Oklahoma City bombing of 1995, still the most deadly case of domestic terrorism in US history, whereas Tywanza Sanders was among 9 people killed in the church shooting in Charleston, South Carolina, in 2015. As so often happens in the case of crimes, particularly those committed by the far right, the perpetrators are humanized in multiple news stories that follow the attack, while the victims are reduced to cold and impersonal statistics.

Last month the FBI released its latest hate crimes statistics, showing a nearly 23% increase in religion-based hate crimes and a 37% spike in anti-Jewish hate crimes in 2017. Almost 60% of victims were targeted because of their (perceived) ethnic or racial identity, some 20% because of their (perceived) religion, almost 16% because of the (perceived) sexuality, and 2% because of their disability or gender. In part because of their definition, hate crimes have a predominantly (far) right wing motivation. However, even in the more neutrally defined case of political violence and terrorism, far-right ideology is the dominant motivation, and far-right terrorism is on the rise.

There is a lot wrong with hate crime statistics, particularly in the US, where no national dataset exists, and even the FBI statistics are

"Race Hate Crimes Are as American as Apple Pie," by Cas Mudde, Guardian News & Media Limited, December 27, 2018. Reprinted by permission.

based on voluntary reporting by local law enforcements agencies, which, in any case, come with all kind of biases. Hence, as is the case with data on sexual violence, among others, hate crime statistics scratch only the surface of the real problem. For example, the National Crime Victimization survey suggested as many as 250,000 annual hate crimes in the period from 2005 to 2015.

Many victims will not report hate crimes for fear of being exposed (ie, homosexuality and undocumented immigrants) or for lack of trust in law enforcement or the criminal justice system (ie, African Americans and Muslims). And even if victims do report hate crimes, many law enforcement agencies will not classify them as such. For example, almost one in five law enforcement agencies did not submit one single hate crime report from 2009 to 2014.

According to the FBI, there were 8,493 victims of hate crimes in the US in 2017. Almost half were victims of intimidation, one-third of "simple assault," and one-fifth of aggravated assault. Most of these people are nothing more than a statistic for both law enforcement and the media. Perhaps their name, age and ethnicity were noted in the story about the hate crime, if it was even reported, but their experience, during and after the crime, were ignored.

Instead, we read about the mitigating factors of the perpetrator, how he was "just an average guy," or "a good neighbor," perhaps withdrawn and with a history of mental health issues—if they were white. The victim is often not just dehumanized by the perpetrator but also by the journalists, reduced to her or his demographics: black, disabled, gay, Jewish, Muslim, or trans.

In a new book, *American Hate: Survivors Speak Out*, community activist and civil rights lawyer Arjun Singh Sethi gives voice to the victims of hate crimes. It is a collection of "testimonials from people impacted by hate before and after the 2016 presidential election."

Letting the people tell their experiences in their own words, *American Hate* gives a face (or better: many faces) to the enduring problem of bigotry and hate crime in this country, highlighting in particular the negative effects of having a "Bigot in Chief" in the White House. Through the stories, it shows the damage done to individuals and communities not just by arson, assault and murder, but also by the less acknowledged cases of everyday bigotry, including bullying, trolling, exclusion, banishment, deprivation, discrimination, stigma, vandalism, and police brutality.

We hear from Taylor Dumpson, the first black women to become student government president at American University, who, reflecting on the horrible racist abuse and intimidation she faced in response to her election, states, "the less we talk about race … the more we fear and hate."

Or from Alexandra Brodsky, a sexual assault survivor who faces anti-Semitism and sexism as she continues to speak out, including about the spike in sexual harassment of girls on school playgrounds by boys who claim that if the president can do it, so can they. Similarly, Harjit Kaur, a Sikh activist and civil rights lawyer whose teen nephew Akal was bullied in school, notes: "Yet today feels worse than 9/11 because our leaders are contributing so openly to this spike in hate." The general mood is captured well by Marwan Kreidie, spokesperson for the Al-Aqsa Islamic Society in Philadelphia: "Most people, including myself, believe we should prepare for the worst and hope for the best."

But what makes this book so powerful, is that it goes beyond the paradigm of (passive and weak) victim, and highlights that they are also (active and strong) survivors. Tanya Gersh, a Jewish citizen of Whitefish, Montana, who is the target of a vicious anti-Semitic campaign by neo-Nazis from around the country, expresses this most powerfully: "Being a victim is painful. But surviving and fighting back has brought me a sense of peace and justice. As long as I'm alive, I want to fight and make sure nobody else endures this again."

Hate crimes are as American as apple pie. As Sethi notes in his introduction to *American Hate*: the US was built on a hate crime, and has a long history of hate crimes, but "the hate nowadays is more visceral and widespread" than in the past decades. As Trump emboldens, empowers, enables, facilitates and legitimizes the perpetrators of hate crimes, we should do the same for its survivors and victims. First and foremost, by putting them central in hate crime accounts and investigations. Second, by humanizing them, rather than reducing them to mere statistics. Third, by giving them a platform to express their experiences in their own words. Or, as Native tribal attorney Ruth Hopkins aptly summarizes: "See us. Hear us. Make sure we are included."

Racism Is Not Based in Genetics

Adam Rutherford

Adam Rutherford is a geneticist and author. He is a presenter for BBC Radio 4's Inside Science *show.*

Barely a week goes by without some dispiriting tale of racism seeping into the public consciousness: the endless stream of Ukip supporters expressing some ill-conceived and unimaginative hate; football hooligans pushing a black man from a train. I am partly of Indian descent, a bit swarthy, and my first experience of racism was more baffling than upsetting. In 1982, my dad, sister and I were at the Co-op in a small village in Suffolk where we lived, when some boys shouted "Coco and Leroy" at us. *Fame* was the big hit on telly at the time, and they were the lead characters. My sister and I thought this was excellent: both amazing dancers and supremely attractive: we did bad splits all the way home.

As someone who writes about evolution and genetics—both of which involve the study of inheritance, and both of which rely on making quantitative comparisons between living things—I often receive letters from people associating Darwin with racism, usually citing the use of the words "favoured races" in the lengthy subtitle to his masterpiece, *On the Origin of Species*. Of course, Darwin doesn't discuss humans in that great book, and "races" was used to describe groups within non-human species. Contemporary use of language must be taken into account.

Darwin was not a racist. He did not, unlike many of his contemporaries, think human "races" might be separate creations. He was a staunch abolitionist, impressed and influenced by his friend and taxidermy tutor John Edmonstone at Edinburgh, who was a freed black slave. However, Darwin's half-cousin Francis Galton most certainly was a racist. He wrote that the Chinese were a race of geniuses, that "Negroes" were vastly inferior, that "Hindoos" were inferior in "strength and business habits" and that the "Arab is little more than an eater up of other men's produce; he is a destroyer."

Obviously, these views are as absurd as they are unacceptable today, as bewildering as calling two half-Indian kids the stage names of two African-American actors. Galton is a problem figure, simultaneously a great scientist and a horror. Among his myriad contributions to science, he invented statistical tools we still use today, and formalised biometrics on humans in new ways. He coined the phrase "nature versus nurture," which has persistently blighted discussions of genetics, implying that these two factors are in conflict, when in fact they are in concert. It was Galton who gave us the word "eugenics," too, an idea that didn't carry the same poisonous stigma it does today. He was enthusiastic about improving the British "stock," prompted by the paucity of healthy recruits for the Boer war.

Many prominent figures were influenced by Galton: Marie Stopes argued forcefully for the compulsory "sterilisation of those unfit for parenthood." Both Theodore Roosevelt and Churchill desired the neutering of the "feeble-minded," as was the parlance in Edwardian days. At University College London, Galton founded the Eugenics Records Office, which became the Galton Laboratory for National Eugenics. By the time I studied there in the 1990s, it had long since dropped that toxic word to become the Galton Laboratory of the Department of Human Genetics.

Genetics has a blighted past with regards to race. Even today, important figures from its history—notably James Watson, co-discoverer of the double helix—express unsupportable racist views. The irony is that while Galton spawned a field with the intention of revealing essential racial differences between the peoples of the Earth, his legacy—human genetics—has shown he was wrong. Most modern geneticists are much less like Galton and more like Darwin. A dreadful book published last year by former *New York Times* science writer Nicholas Wade espoused views about racial differences seemingly backed by genetics. As with Watson, the reaction from geneticists was uniformly dismissive, that he had failed to understand the field, and misrepresented their work.

We now know that the way we talk about race has no scientific validity. There is no genetic basis that corresponds with any particular group of people, no essentialist DNA for black people or white people or anyone. This is not a hippy ideal, it's a fact. There are genetic characteristics that associate with certain populations, but none of these is exclusive, nor correspond uniquely with any one group that might fit a racial epithet. Regional adaptations are real, but these tend to express difference within so-called races, not between them. Sickle-cell anaemia affects people of all skin colours because it has evolved where malaria is common. Tibetans are genetically adapted to high altitude, rendering Chinese residents of Beijing more similar to Europeans than their superficially similar neighbours. Tay-Sachs disease, once thought to be a "Jewish disease," is as common in French Canadians and Cajuns. And so it goes on.

We harvest thousands of human genomes every week. Last month, the UK launched the 100,000 Genomes project to identify genetic bases for many diseases, but within that booty we will also find more of the secret history of our species, our DNA mixed and remixed through endless sex and continuous migration. We are too horny and mobile to have stuck to our own kind for very long.

Race doesn't exist, racism does. But we can now confine it to opinions and not pretend that there might be any scientific validity in bigotry.

Implicit Biases Are Shaped by Our Environments

American Bar Association Commission on Disability Rights

The American Bar Association (ABA) Commission on Disability Rights works to promote the American Bar Association's commitment to justice and rule of law for people with mental, physical, and sensory disabilities, and to promote their full and equal participation in the legal profession.

Most of us believe that we are fair and equitable, and evaluate others based on objective facts. However, all of us, even the most egalitarian, have implicit biases—also referred to as unconscious biases or implicit social cognition. They are triggered automatically, in about a tenth of a second, without our conscious awareness or intention, and cause us to have attitudes about and preferences for people based on characteristics such as age, gender, race, ethnicity, sexual orientation, disability, and religion. These implicit biases often do not reflect or align with our conscious, declared beliefs. Notably, they influence our decisions and actions and can predict our behavior.

Implicit biases about persons with disabilities are pervasive. One study found that "[p]reference for people without disability compared to people with disabilities was among the strongest implicit and explicit effects across the social group domains" (e.g., gender, race, religion, sexuality, weight, political orientation, etc.), with only age showing more implicit bias. Significantly, 76 percent of respondents showed an implicit preference for people without disabilities, compared to nine percent for people with disabilities. Even test takers with disabilities showed a preference for people without disabilities.

"Implicit Biases & People with Disabilities," American Bar Association, January 7, 2019. Reprinted by permission.

The American Bar Association's Commission on Disability Rights has created this resource to increase awareness of implicit biases, both in general and in particular with regard to persons with disabilities, and to offer techniques to help mitigate these biases. We begin with an overview of implicit bias, in particular what is implicit bias, where do such biases originate, how can we measure them, why are they harmful, and how can we mitigate them. This is followed by a series of questions and scenarios that will allow you to examine your implicit biases about persons with disabilities.

Overview

What Is Implicit Bias?

Implicit or unconscious bias is defined as "the process of associating stereotypes or attitudes toward categories of people without our conscious awareness."

All of us have a natural human tendency to sort people into groups based on characteristics such as age, gender, race, ethnicity, sexual orientation, disability, and religion. These unconscious responses allow our brain to process vast amounts of information about one another at lightning speed. We process approximately 200,000 times more information each second unconsciously than consciously. Having to process everything about each person we meet would be both overwhelming and likely incapacitating. Sorting is a type of cognitive shorthand.

We then associate feelings and traits, both positive and negative, with anyone categorized as being from a particular group. We pay attention to facts that confirm our associations and ignore or screen out facts that contradict them. We tend to see an individual as a representation of a particular group rather than as an individual.

Further, we tend to favor, prefer, and associate positive characteristics with members of the group to which we belong—people who are like us. This is known as in-group favoritism or in-group bias. All of us belong to cultural groups defined by traits such as race, ethnicity, religion, gender, disability, sexual orientation, national origin, family, or social or professional status. In-group bias is so strong that, even when randomly assigned to a group, people report a preference for that group. Accordingly, we tend to associate negative characteristics with or disfavor members of groups to which we do not belong. This is referred to as out-group bias. All of these tendencies are the foundation of stereotyping, prejudice and, ultimately, may result in discriminatory decisions or actions, even if those decisions or actions might not be what we consciously intend or acknowledge.

Where Do Implicit Biases Originate?
Implicit biases are shaped by our personal experiences, the attitudes of family, friends and others, living and working environments, culture, the media, movies, and books. Implicit biases develop over the course of a lifetime, beginning at an early age.

How Can We Measure Implicit Biases?
It used to be that if we wanted to know a person's biases, we asked. However, we now know that self-reports of biases are unreliable due, in part, to the fact that we are often unaware of our biases, believe we are not biased, or may modify our responses to align with what is regarded as socially acceptable. The Implicit Association Test (IAT) is one of the most well-known, popular, and widely used tools for measuring one's implicit biases, and has been responsible for introducing the concept of implicit bias to the public. There are numerous IATs (over 90) that assess implicit biases across a wide range of characteristics, including race, disability, sexuality, age, gender, career, religion, and weight.

Introduced in 1998 and maintained by Project Implicit—a consortium comprised of researchers from Harvard University, the University of Virginia, and the University of Washington—the IAT is a web-based test that measures the strength of associations between concepts (e.g., "Disabled Persons," "Abled Persons") and evaluations (e.g., "Bad," "Good"). Test takers are asked to quickly sort words and images/symbols into categories (e.g., Good, Bad, Disabled Persons, Abled Persons) by pressing the "e" key if the word or image/symbol belongs to the category on the left, and the "i" key if the word or image/symbol belongs to the category on the right.

An individual's IAT score is based on how long it takes (speed) the individual, on average, to sort words and images/symbols when the categories are combined, such as Good or Disabled Persons and Bad or Abled Persons and vice versa. The IAT recognizes that most of us identify words and images or symbols more quickly when they originate from what we perceive as closely related rather than unrelated categories. For example, if you are faster to categorize words when "Disabled Persons and Good" share a response relative to when "Disabled Persons and Bad" share a response key, you would have an implicit preference for "Disabled Persons."

How Are Implicit Biases Harmful?

Implicit biases influence our perceptions, judgments, decisions, and actions and can predict behavior. Implicit biases can lead to microaggressions. These subtle, but offensive comments or actions, which are often unintentional and reflect implicit biases, unconsciously reinforce a stereotype when directed at persons based on their membership in a marginalized group. Unlike explicit discrimination, microaggressions typically are committed by people who are well-meaning. For example, a waiter may ask the person accompanying a blind person or wheelchair user what he or she would like to order, sending the message that a person with a disability is unable to make decisions independently. These "small" slights are cumulative and significant over time.

Social scientists point to mounting evidence that implicit biases can lead to discriminatory actions in a wide range of human interactions, from education to employment, health care, housing, and criminal justice. When we look at some of the disproportionalities (i.e., the differences between a group's representation in the population at large and its over- or under-representation in specific areas) that have plagued us for so long, despite society's best intentions, it is hard to explain them.

For example, we know that students with disabilities achieve in school at a lower rate than others and are far more often and more severely disciplined in school. Most of us believe that teachers and school administrators act in good faith and have good intentions. If we were to ask them whether they intentionally and explicitly intend to treat students with disabilities with lower expectations and discipline them more severely than students without disabilities, most if not all would say that was not their intent, and believe that they are making decisions based on objective facts. Yet, it is difficult to understand the disproportionate results. One possible explanation is that these decision-makers are indeed acting in good faith, but are responding with implicit biases.

How Can We Mitigate Unconscious Biases?

Acknowledging the difficulties of controlling biases that are unconscious and automatic, the good news is that implicit biases are malleable and their effect on behavior can be managed and mitigated. Although nearly all of us have implicit biases, we can take steps to minimize how often they are activated and how much they affect our perceptions, decisions, and actions. The first step is to acknowledge that we have implicit biases. To learn what those are, we can take the Implicit Association Test or other tests that measure implicit responses. Once aware, motivation to change and to manage your biases is critical.

Researchers have developed various de-biasing interventions to counter the negative effects of implicit biases by building new mental associations. To reinforce these new associations, these interventions must be consistently and continuously reapplied. These interventions include:

- **Intergroup Contact:** Meet and engage with individual members of outgroups. Getting to know people one-on-one and engaging in positive meaningful relationships can help you build new positive associations and reduce stereotyping.
- **Counter-stereotypes:** Develop new associations that counter your stereotypes. Expose yourself to or think about exemplars

who possess positive traits that contrast with your stereotypes. For example, read about blind judge Richard Bernstein who sits on the Michigan Supreme Court.

- **Individuation:** Consider the attributes of the individual apart from his or her group. For instance, when you meet someone who has a mental health condition, focus on his or her individual characteristics, traits, interests, and preferences rather than stereotypes about persons with these conditions.
- **Perspective Taking:** Take the perspective of the person. Try to understand from their perspective what they encounter and what adaptive techniques they might use to function successfully.
- **Deliberative Processing:** Reflect on your perceptions, judgments, behavior, decisions, and actions to better understand which ones are worthy of a more thoughtful consideration rather than a split-second reaction. We tend to act on our stereotypes when we have a lot of information to process in a short amount of time and feel stressed.
- **Common Ground:** Focus on what you have in common with the individual members of the groups you are stereotyping.
- **Education:** Participate in trainings and other educational programs aimed at raising awareness about implicit biases and their impact.
- **Self-Monitoring:** Continuously self-monitor your perceptions, judgments, behavior, decisions, and actions for the influence of implicit biases.
- **Accountability:** Hold yourself responsible for the negative influence that implicit biases have on your perceptions, judgments, behavior, decisions, and actions. Do not dismiss your accountability simply because implicit biases are triggered automatically without our conscious awareness.

Implicit Disability Biases: Questions to Ask Yourself

Reflect on each of the questions below. Consider whether and to what extent your response may be influenced by stereotypes and biases about people with disabilities and/or informed by objective facts and evidence and actual experiences with them.

1. When you think of a person with a disability, do you focus on the things the person can do or cannot do? Where do you get the information on which you base your views? Did you ask or observe the person with a disability?

2. Do you think of a person with a disability as working in certain careers? If so, which careers and why?

3. When you think of a person with a disability, do you have sympathy or feel pity for the person?

4. When you meet a person with a disability, do you see the person's disability before you see the person?

5. Do you think about people with disabilities as a group or as individuals? If as a group, what characteristics do you think people with disabilities share?

6. Do you consider people with disabilities as different from people without disabilities? If so, how are they different?

7. Do you believe that the lives of people with disabilities are different from the lives of people without disabilities? If so, how are they different?

8. Do you use terms (e.g., "normal" or "able-bodied") to differentiate between people without disabilities and people with disabilities?

9. Do you speak to and interact with people with disabilities differently than you do with people without disabilities? If so, how and why?

10. Do you perceive people with disabilities as dependent compared to people without disabilities? Do you base your belief on personal experiences or other sources? If the latter, what are the sources?

11. Would you describe persons with disabilities as brave, courageous, inspirational, superhuman, and heroic? If so, why?

12. Do you perceive people with disabilities as productive or competent as people without disabilities? If so, why?

13. Do you view people with disabilities as too costly for employers to hire? If so, please explain.

14. Do you view disability as an abnormality or sickness or as a challenge that needs to be overcome or corrected? When you see a person with a disability, do you automatically want to help them?

15. Do you think workers with disabilities receive special advantages or are held to a lesser standard than workers without disabilities?

Specific Disabilities

1. Do you perceive persons with mental illness as violent or dangerous? If so, based on what information?

2. Do you view people with intellectual disabilities or developmental disabilities as being dependent on others to care for them? As being kind and generous? As being innocent and sweet-natured?

3. Do you think all blind people have a keener sense of smell and hearing?

4. Do you think people with cerebral palsy have cognitive impairments as well?

5. Do you view people with hidden impairments such as learning disabilities, arthritis, and heart conditions as having a disability?

6. Do you think all blind people read braille?

Scenarios for Discussion

Scenario 1

Nicole, who uses a wheelchair for mobility, is interviewing for an associate position in the litigation department at a "big law" firm. The partner asks Nicole whether she has considered working in other departments that do not involve going to court, and whether she is able to represent clients effectively in court. Nicole responds that her passion is litigation, pointing out that she won several moot court competitions and has courtroom experience through a pro bono project and a legal aid clinic. The partner informs Nicole that he would initially meet with her clients to ensure that they are comfortable being represented by an attorney in a wheelchair.

What implicit biases does the partner have about Nicole?

What message is the partner sending her?

What message is given to clients if the partner proceeds as he suggests?

What could the partner have done differently?

What questions are appropriate to ask in this situation?

Scenario 2

Robert, who has depression, works at a large public relations firm. At times, his depression worsens. When this occurs, he requests a flexible schedule—to arrive at work late rather than early morning—as an accommodation. Robert's supervisor assembles a team to work on an important project for the firm. She decides, based on the long hours this will require, the numerous tight deadlines that need to be met, and the team meetings involved, not to assign Robert.

What assumptions did the supervisor make about Robert's abilities?

Were the supervisor's reasons for not including Robert on the team reasonable?

What questions should the supervisor have asked Robert before making her decision?

Scenario 3

Judge Thompson is presiding over a custody battle involving three-year-old Sean. The boy's mother is blind, and his father does not have any disabilities. Judge Thompson must determine the best interests of Sean, namely what environment will foster and encourage his happiness, safety, mental health, and development.

What factors should the judge consider in making his decision?

Does being blind necessarily impact the mother's parenting capacity? If so, how?

What types of evidence should Sean's mother present?

What types of evidence should Sean's father present?

Science Does Not Excuse Bigotry, but It Can Be Used to Fight It

Adam Rutherford

Adam Rutherford is a geneticist and author. He is a presenter for BBC Radio 4's Inside Science *show.*

It seems we can't move for comments about race dominating our media landscape, be it about an actor formerly known as a princess, or by an actor previously unknown to anyone outside of his famous acting dynasty. These are fractious times, and such debates appear to be increasing in frequency. But there are some fights for which you can arm yourself in advance—and when the argument is about race, the weapon of choice is science.

Racism is a prejudice that has a longstanding relationship with science. The invention of race occurred in the age of empires and plunder, when men of the emerging discipline of science classified the people of the world, mostly from their armchairs. Carl Linnaeus is the father of biological taxonomy, having invented the system that we use today: genus and species—*Homo sapiens*. He was also a central figure in the emergence of scientific racism too, alongside Kant, Voltaire and a host of other European men.

Classifications were based primarily on skin colour, some on a handful of skull measurements, and they also came with some shoddy value judgments: Linnaeus had the people of Africa as lazy and "governed by caprice"; Native Americans were "zealous and stubborn"; East Asians were haughty, greedy, and "ruled by opinions." Voltaire believed that black people were a different species. All of these taxonomies were inherently hierarchical, with white Europeans always on top.

In the 19th century, Darwin's half-cousin Francis Galton and others tightened their scientific arguments for race though, as

"How to Fight Racism Using Science," by Adam Rutherford, Guardian News & Media Limited, January 26, 2020. Reprinted by permission.

Darwin noted, no one could agree on how many races there actually were, the range being between one and 63. Galton was an amazing scientist, and a stunning racist. The most delicious irony about him is that the field he effectively established—human genetics—is the branch of science that has demonstrated unequivocally that race is not biologically meaningful. Modern genetics clearly shows that the way we colloquially define race does not align with the biology that underpins human variation. Instead, race is a cultural taxonomy—a social construct. This doesn't mean it is invalid or unimportant, nor does it mean that race does not exist. Humans are social animals, and the way we perceive each other is of paramount importance. Race exists because we perceive it.

Racism seems to be making a comeback in public life: the prime minister has a well-stocked back catalogue of racist remarks, most notably describing Congolese people as "piccanninies" with "watermelon smiles." Antisemitism is a defining issue for the 21st-century Labour party. Sport has always suffered from racist fans, and in 2018, bananas were thrown on to pitches at black footballers such as Arsenal's Pierre-Emerick Aubameyang, as they were routinely 30 years ago. The England cricketer Jofra Archer was subjected to racist abuse in a Test match in New Zealand in November.

We all know someone who has casually racist opinions: the misattribution of elite athletic success to ancestry rather than training, that east Asian students are naturally better at maths, or that Jews are innately good with money. Racism may be back, so get tooled up, because science is no ally to racists. Here are some standard canards of prejudice, and why science says something different.

Skin in the Game

What we see with our eyes is the merest fraction of a person. But humans are a highly visual species, and skin colour is the primary factor in allocating race. This idea is modern though, only becoming the primary classifier during the so-called

Age of Enlightenment. Modern genetics reveals a much more complicated—and fascinating—picture.

Lighter skin is, at least partially, an adaptation to less sunny skies, as a means of protecting us from folate deficiency. *Homo sapiens* originated as an African species, but that doesn't necessarily mean that we were ancestrally dark-skinned, nor that everyone was the same colour. Some of the differences we can see and measure between populations are local adaptations to evolutionary pressures such as food availability and disease. Similarly, genes for lighter pigmentation have been selected by an evolution away from the equator. But the palette of skin colour within the African continent is far greater than anywhere else, meaning that a simplistic model of selection based on exposure to the sun only explains a fraction of that diversity. There are 1.3 billion Africans, 42 million African Americans. Not only are these huge numbers, but the people in question are more diverse genetically than anyone else on Earth. And yet westerners refer to all of them as "black." This is a scientifically meaningless classification, and one that is baked into western culture from five centuries of scientific racism. Stereotyping based on pigmentation is foolish, because racial differences are skin deep.

These Lands Are Your Lands

"England for the English" warbled Morrissey in his song *The National Front Disco*. Now that Mozza has given apparent support to For Britain, a political party even Nigel Farage thinks is full of "Nazis and racists," it's no longer clear the lyrics were ironic. Although Morrissey denies he is a racist, the sentiment is an old racist refrain. In July last year, President Trump suggested that if four elected US congresswomen didn't like it in the US, they should go back to where they came from. Three of them were born in the United States and one is a Somali-born American citizen. Meanwhile, Trump's paternal grandparents were German immigrants, his mother Scottish-born, his first wife Moravian, his third, Slovenian. It is never clear where the benchmark for indigeneity lies.

Indigeneity is a tricky concept. The British Isles have been invaded throughout their history: 1066 was the most recent hostile conquest, but before that, we were occupied by Vikings, who followed Angles, Saxons, Alans, and dozens of other tribes. The Romans ruled for a while, with conscripts not from Rome but from all over their empire, including Gaul, the Mediterranean and sub-Saharan Africa.

About 4,500 years ago, Britain was populated primarily with farmers who had European ancestors. DNA taken from the bones of the long dead suggests they were probably olive-skinned, with dark hair and brown eyes.

The Beaker folk arrived in Britain about 4,400 years ago, and again according to ancient DNA, within a few centuries had replaced almost the entire population. We don't know how or why, whether it was violence, disease, or something else.

Before them there were darker-skinned hunter-gatherers, who had been there a few thousand years. Then it all gets a bit foggy. The earliest evidence of British humans is in the crumbling coastline of Happisburgh in Norfolk, where size nine footprints of an unknown species of human were set in soft stone 900,000 years ago.

No country, people, political power or border is permanent. The only true indigenous Brits were not even our own species. So, when racists say "England for the English," or when they talk about indigenous people, I do not know who they mean, or more specifically, when they mean. They probably don't either.

Pure Blood

White supremacists are obsessed with DNA. I spend time lurking in some of the nastiest corners of the internet, partially so that you don't have to, but also to track their conversations about ancestry. Racist online cesspits such as Stormfront and 4Chan and 8Kun are flooded with thousands of posts about racial purity and ancestry-testing products. Occasionally, these commercial kits reveal previously unknown ancestry from people that white supremacists loathe. White purity is the key idea within white supremacy, and reactions are often conspiracy-fuelled ("the companies are owned by Jews"), or just absurd: "When you look in the mirror, do you see a jew [sic]? If not, you're good," which somewhat undermines the point of the tests.

There are no purebred humans. Our family trees are matted webs, and all lines of our ancestry get tangled after a few generations. All Nazis have Jewish forebears, all racists have African ancestors. Non-racists often think that their ancestry is somehow pure too, and this can be bolstered by misinterpreting commercial genetic ancestry kits. But no matter how isolated or wholesome you think your family tree is, it is a node on a tangled bank, linked directly to everyone else on your continent after only a few centuries, and everyone in the world after a couple of millennia.

Genealogy and genetic genealogy are not perfectly aligned, and due to the way DNA is shuffled during the production of sperm and egg, much is cumulatively lost over the generations. What this means is that you carry DNA from only half of your ancestors 11 generations back. You are genetically unrelated to people from whom you are actually descended as recently as the middle of the 18th century. You are descended from multitudes, most of whom you know nothing about, and many of whom you have no meaningful genetic relationship with.

Black Power

The last white man to win the 100m final at the Olympics was Allan Wells in 1980, a year when the US boycotted the event. This was also the last time white men competed in the final, five in total. For many, this forms the basis of a long-standing assumption that black people—and more specifically African Americans, Jamaicans or Canadians—have a biological advantage for explosive energy sports.

Unfortunately, elite sportspeople are an abysmal sample on which to make generalisations about populations—they are already wonderfully freakish outliers. The sample size is hopeless, too: the total number of athletes that have competed in the 100m Olympic final since Wells took the gold is 58. Five of them were African, and not from the west African countries from where the enslaved were taken. By this metric, Africans are exactly as successful as white people in the 100m since 1980.

The argument that informs this misguided idea is that centuries of slavery have resulted in selection for explosive energy genes (about which we know very little). This is also a total nonstarter, for many reasons. Most significantly, we can look for the signals of evolutionary selection in African Americans since the beginning of transatlantic slavery, that is, genes that have proliferated in that population. A 2014 study of the DNA of 29,141 African Americans showed no signs of selection across the whole genome for any trait in the time since their ancestors were taken from their African homelands.

But for the sake of argument, let's pretend that genes were selected that related to power and strength. Why then do eastern Europeans dominate weightlifting, yet are absent from sprinting? Why do African Americans dominate in boxing, but not wrestling? Where are all the black sprint cyclists? Why is it that in the 50m freestyle in swimming in the whole history of the Olympics, the number of African American finalists is… one? None of these facts align with the slavery explanation for African American dominance in the 100m.

The transatlantic slave trade also imported millions of West African people to South America. The number of South Americans of any ancestry to have competed in the 100m finals? Zero.

The point is this: sprinters in the Olympics, or indeed any elite sportspeople, are not a dataset on which a statistician could draw any satisfactory conclusion. Yet it is precisely the data on which extremely popular racial stereotypes are based. Elite athletes deserve better praise than the belief that they have auspicious ancestry.

Hate Is a Biological Survival Mechanism

Crissy Milazzo

Crissy Milazzo is a freelance writer and copy editor based in Los Angeles.

If you've ever unfriended someone on Facebook or muted a person on Twitter, then you understand what it's like to viscerally dislike a person. Although these tools give us an "out of sight, out of mind" way to cleanse our lives of what we don't want to see, we can never truly avoid the feeling of "dislike" altogether.

Indeed, dislike is a necessary survival mechanism that humans have been using to get by for centuries, way before the jungle of social media took over. Here's how the mind-body connection involved in disliking someone works.

The Response in the Body When We Dislike Someone

In order to understand what happens in your body when you dislike someone, you can start by trying to understand fear. As Robert Sapolsky writes in "Why Your Brain Hates Other People," when we see someone who even looks different from us, "there is preferential activation of the amygdala," which means the brain region associated with fear and aggression flares up. This visceral, emotional reaction can spark a long-term pattern of dislike when it's validated by action: if you perceive that someone has hurt you, your fear of them becomes rational.

Our negative feelings toward someone get stronger as bad experiences with them pile up, and these negative thoughts trigger the fight-or-flight response in our bodies. As AJ Marsden, assistant professor of psychology at Beacon College in Leesburg, Florida,

"What Happens in the Brain When We Dislike Somebody," by Crissy Milazzo, HEADSPACE INC. Reprinted by permission.

puts it, "our fight-or-flight response is our bodies way of dealing with a stressor."

Stressors that trigger fight-or-flight need not be life or death, though, says Marsden: "Sadly, our body cannot tell the difference between an actual stressor (being chased by someone with a knife) and a perceived stressor (having to work with someone you hate)." This is why seeing posts from your high school bully can make you feel the anxiety of being bullied all over again: your fearful associations with disliking the person trigger your own need to protect yourself.

Negative Feelings Put Stress on Our Bodies

Over time, this response puts stress on our bodies, conditioning us to be more skeptical of a person's actions than we would be if we felt neutral about them. "In the mind, the neural connections become stronger and cause us to dwell more on the negative aspects of that person," says Marsden. "Even if they were to do something positive, we'd pay more attention to the negative because that's what we've trained our brain to do." This explains why we have a seemingly endless list of negative facts about people we dislike, even if our rational brain would tell us there has to be something redeeming about them.

This heightened arousal of our fearful instincts causes us to dread future interactions with people we dislike. In turn, this conditions us into even further dislike of that person, which just validates our negative feelings. In this way, our distaste for another person becomes like a snake eating its tail: we dislike them because they make us feel bad, and we feel bad because we dislike them.

How to Overcome Our Dislike

But since there's no "Black Mirror"-style real life-muting feature, we have to learn how to overcome dislike in order to get on with our daily lives. As Marsden points out, our dislike has a tendency to negatively impact our own behavior with co-workers and mutual friends: "If we don't like a person, we may be short with them or interrupt them without realizing it. They notice our rudeness toward them and often respond with rudeness, confirming our negative thoughts about that person."

The key to breaking this vicious cycle, Marsden says, is mindfulness; when you're aware of how your dislike influences your body (and your behavior), you can start to condition yourself to respond rationally. When it comes to dislike, maybe "out of sight, out of mind, out of control" is a better-amended motto. Since dislike is rooted in a fear of the unknown, perhaps understanding more about where our dislike comes from can help us overcome its influence on our behavior.

And when all else fails, there's always the "block" feature.

Aggressive Speech Primes the Brain for Hateful Actions

Arthur Glenberg

Arthur Glenberg is a professor of psychology at Arizona State University and a professor emeritus at the University of Wisconsin–Madison. His research covers cognitive psychology and cognitive neuroscience with a focus on developing theories of embodied cognition in language, education, and social processes.

A mark on a page, an online meme, a fleeting sound. How can these seemingly insignificant stimuli lead to acts as momentous as participation in a racist rally or the massacre of innocent worshippers? Psychologists, neuroscientists, linguists and philosophers are developing a new theory of language understanding that's starting to provide answers.

Current research shows that humans understand language by activating sensory, motor and emotional systems in the brain. According to this new simulation theory, just reading words on a screen or listening to a podcast activates areas of the brain in ways similar to the activity generated by literally being in the situation the language describes. This process makes it all the more easy to turn words into actions.

As a cognitive psychologist, my own research has focused on developing simulation theory, testing it, and using it to create reading comprehension interventions for young children.

Simulations Are Step One

Traditionally, linguists have analyzed language as a set of words and rules that convey ideas. But how do ideas become actions?

Simulation theory tries to answer that question. In contrast, many traditional theories about language processing give action short shrift.

Simulation theory proposes that processing words depends on activity in people's neural and behavioral systems of action, perception and emotion. The idea is that perceiving words drives your brain systems into states that are nearly identical to what would be evoked by directly experiencing what the words describe.

Consider the sentence "The lovers held hands while they walked along the moonlit tropical beach." According to simulation theory, when you read these words, your brain's motor system simulates the actions of walking; that is, the neural activity elicited by comprehending the words is similar to the neural activity generated by literal walking. Similarly, your brain's perceptual systems simulate the sight, sounds and feel of the beach. And your emotional system simulates the feelings implied by the sentence.

So words themselves are enough to trigger simulations in motor, perceptual and emotional neural systems. Your brain creates a sense of being there: The motor system is primed for action and the emotional system motivates those actions.

Then, one can act on the simulation much as he'd act in the real situation. For example, language associating an ethnic group with "bad hombres" could invoke an emotional simulation upon seeing members of the group. If that emotional reaction is strong enough, it may in turn motivate action—maybe making a derogatory remark or physically lashing out.

Although simulation theory is still under scientific scrutiny, there have been many successful tests of its predictions. For example, using neuroimaging techniques that track blood flow in the brain, researchers found that listening to action words such as "lick," "pick" and "kick" produces activity in areas of the brain's motor cortex that are used to control the mouth, the hand and the leg, respectively. Hearing a sentence such as "The ranger saw an eagle in the sky" generates a mental image using the visual cortex. And using Botox to block activity in the muscles that furrow the brow affects the emotional system and slows understanding of sentences conveying angry content. These examples demonstrate the connections between processing speech and motor, sensory and emotional systems.

Recently, my colleague psychologist Michael McBeath, our graduate student Christine S. P. Yu and I discovered yet another robust connection between language and the emotional system.

Consider pairs of single-syllable English words that differ only in whether the vowel sound is "eee" or "uh," such as "gleam-glum" and "seek-suck." Using all such pairs in English—there are about 90 of them—we asked people to judge which word in the pair was more positive. Participants selected the word with the "eee" sound two-thirds of the time. This is a remarkable percentage because if linguistic sounds and emotions were unrelated and people were picking at the rate of chance, only half of the "eee" words would have been judged as the more positive.

We propose that this relation arose because saying "eee" activates the same muscles and neural systems as used when smiling—or saying "cheese!" In fact, mechanically inducing a smile—as by holding a pencil in your teeth without using your lips—lightens your mood. Our new research shows that saying words that use the smile muscles can have a similar effect.

We tested this idea by having people chew gum while judging the words. Chewing gum blocks the systematic activation of the smile muscles. Sure enough, while chewing gum, the judged difference between the "eee" and "uh" words was only half as strong. We also demonstrated the same effects in China using pairs of Mandarin words containing the "eee" and "uh" sounds.

Practice Through Simulation Makes Actions Easier

Of course, motivating someone to commit a hate crime requires much more than uttering "glum" or "suck."

But consider that simulations become quicker with repetition. When one first hears a new word or concept, creating its simulation can be a mentally laborious process. A good communicator can help by using hand gestures to convey the motor simulation, pointing to objects or pictures to help create the perceptual simulation and using facial expressions and voice modulation to induce the emotional simulation.

It makes sense that the echo chamber of social media provides the practice needed to both speed and shape the simulation. The mental simulation of "caravan" can change from an emotionally neutral string of camels to an emotionally charged horde of drug dealers and rapists. And, through the repeated simulation that comes from repeatedly reading similar posts, the message becomes all the more believable, as each repetition produces another instance of almost being there to see it with your own eyes.

Psycholinguist Dan Slobin suggested that habitual ways of speaking lead to habitual ways of thinking about the world. The language that you hear gives you a vocabulary for discussing the world, and that vocabulary, by producing simulations, gives you habits of mind. Just as reading a scary book can make you afraid to go in the ocean because you simulate (exceedingly rare) shark attacks, encountering language about other groups of people (and their exceedingly rare criminal behavior) can lead to a skewed view of reality.

Practice need not always lead down an emotional rabbit hole, though, because alternative simulations and understandings can be created. A caravan can be simulated as families in distress who have the grit, energy and skills to start a new life and enrich new communities.

Because simulation creates a sense of being in a situation, it motivates the same actions as the situation itself. Simulating fear and anger literally makes you fearful and angry and promotes aggression. Simulating compassion and empathy literally makes you act kindly. We all have the obligation to think critically and to speak words that become humane actions.

CONTROVERSIES

CHAPTER 2

Is It Useful to Label and Monitor Hate Groups?

Overview: There Are Many Ways for Hate Groups to Form and Proliferate

Anti-Defamation League

The Anti-Defamation League (ADL) is an international non-governmental organization based in the US. It works to oppose extremism and anti-Semitism.

There are hundreds of white supremacist groups in the United States, from Ku Klux Klan organizations to racist skinhead gangs. Most white supremacists don't actually belong to organized groups, but hate groups provide white supremacists with most of the propaganda, ideology and motivation to act for the whole movement, and are highly visible examples of America's white supremacy problem.

So how do these hate groups form? The answer to that question isn't as simple as one might think. In the most basic sense, an extremist group can emerge when one or more individuals devoted to a certain cause recruit other like-minded individuals to form an organized group. In reality, there are usually many complicating factors that affect group formation.

Some extremist movements are more interested in group formation than other, more loosely organized movements. Moreover, the Internet allows extremists to share ideas and strategies easily without people even needing to be involved with a specific group. In some cases, though, the speed and breadth of communication allowed by the Internet can assist group formation.

A new movement is much more likely to form groups by imitating other recently formed groups (see copycatting, below). Group formation in a mature extremist movement is different, because of the presence and effects of all the other, pre-existing groups.

"How Hate Groups Form," Anti-Defamation League. Published with permission of the Anti-Defamation League, New York, NY. All rights reserved.

The white supremacist movement is an example of a mature extremist movement with a number of major subsets, from neo-Nazis to white supremacist prison gangs. As a result, group creation within the white supremacist movement can take a number of different forms or, in some cases, combinations of forms.

Here are the eight most common ways white supremacists currently form hate groups in the United States:

1. Graduation

Probably the most frequent way hate groups form is through a process that can be called graduation: when a white supremacist decides to form their own group after having previously spent time as a member of one or more previous hate groups. Having learned about extremism in the original group, the "graduated" extremist then recruits members from the broader white supremacist movement.

Graduation can occur through ambition, when white supremacists seek more status than their current group allows, or through rejection, when they have been expelled from a group. Billy Roper is a good example. A longstanding Arkansas white supremacist who currently heads a small group dubbed the Shield Wall Network, Roper was involved with several white supremacist groups in the 1990s and early 2000s, including the neo-Nazi National Alliance, before disagreements with other National Alliance members caused him to leave that group and form White Revolution. When that group failed, Roper became involved with a Ku Klux Klan group before eventually venturing out again to create the Shield Wall Network.

Groups formed by people with organizational or leadership skills can have considerable staying power compared to other white supremacist groups. Some of the more notorious white supremacist groups in recent American history, such as Aryan Nations and the National Alliance, are good examples of this. However, individuals with true leadership skills are in short supply in today's white supremacist movement.

One variation on this theme occurs when the "graduate" specifically recruits from members of existing groups of the same type, rather than from the white supremacist movement at large or the general public.

This process, sometimes called cannibalization, is particularly common among Ku Klux Klan groups but can also be found among other types of groups. If a new Klan group's membership grows, it is often only because it is drawing members away from other, existing Klan groups—and, in turn, the new group's membership can easily be lured away by an even newer group. This is one reason why most Klan groups in the United States today are only a few years old and why new Klan groups keep forming without increasing the total number of Klan group members.

2. Off-shooting

Another common way hate groups form is through off-shooting, which occurs when members of an organization break away to form their own group, often intended to rival or resemble the original entity. White supremacist groups tend to be fractious and susceptible to splintering, which results in new, smaller groups. In the early 2000s, for example, some members of the Hammerskins racist skinhead group broke off to form the Outlaw Hammerskins. More recently, members of the new neo-Nazi group Vanguard America broke away to form the rival groups, Patriot Front and National Socialist Legion.

Sometimes offshoots form as a result of personal conflicts, but in other cases off-shooting may occur because the original group is deemed insufficiently active or radical. In fact, in some cases the original group may not even be white supremacist in nature. For example, several white supremacist groups have been formed over the years by people who had joined other right-wing groups, such as the John Birch Society, only to become disappointed at the lack of explicit racism or anti-Semitism in such groups. They then leave to form their own more radical, more openly racist organizations.

3. Factionalization

Factionalization occurs when an entire group disintegrates into smaller, squabbling factions. In the 2000s, following the deaths of their longstanding leaders, the memberships of two neo-Nazi groups, the National Alliance and Aryan Nations, each split into several different factions that claimed to be the true successor group. Most of the factions lasted only a few years before themselves collapsing.

4. Resurrection

Defunct hate groups don't always stay defunct. Groups can form when white supremacists attempt to resurrect a defunct but previously well-known group because it has a "brand name" power within the white supremacist movement. The white supremacists attempting the resurrection are often but not always former members of the group.

The single most successful example of resurrection in the history of white supremacy involved the Ku Klux Klan. The original Ku Klux Klan faded away in the 1870s, but decades later, a revival of the group experienced phenomenal success and growth, with the Second Ku Klux Klan expanding to millions of members by the early 1920s. Scandals and bad publicity caused it to decline afterwards. A success on that scale is not likely to happen again.

A more recent Klan example involves the United Klans of America (UKA). Half a century ago, the UKA was one of the largest and most notorious Klan groups in the United States, linked to a number of murders and other acts of violence. It collapsed in the 1980s after being sued by the Southern Poverty Law Center. After a failed attempt in the 1990s to resurrect the group, a longstanding Alabama Klan figure, Bradley Jenkins, tried again in 2015.

After its aforementioned split, Aryan Nations also experienced attempts at resurrection, including an effort to recast it as a biker group dubbed Aryan Nations Sadistic Souls. The Sadistic Souls claim to be the true successor to Aryan Nations because one of its members says he is the nephew of the original group's founder.

5. Subcultural Groups

American society contains many subcultures—people with shared dress, rituals, language, music and more. Occasionally a subculture will be exposed to white supremacist ideology and parts of it may start to incorporate that ideology into its own subcultural activities—including the formation of groups within that subculture. The most famous example of this sort of evolution occurred in Great Britain in the 1970s, when the skinhead subculture developed a racist variant. By the 1980s, that strain had found its way to the United States, where many racist skinhead groups subsequently formed.

Similarly, some white supremacist gangs emerged from the 1980s California punk scene. Some, such as Public Enemy Number One (PEN1), still exist today, though the present-day gang—essentially a white supremacist prison gang—bears little resemblance to its original iteration.

Today, the alt right segment of the white supremacist movement is a similar example of subcultural emergence. The alt right evolved from a variety of beliefs and subcultures, most significantly the online gaming subculture, the misogynistic subculture of the "manosphere," and the imageboard subculture of sites like 4chan and 8chan.

To date, the alt right has not tended strongly towards group formation—probably a relic of its online origins—but groups that have emerged carry the DNA of their foundational subcultures.

Just as hate groups can evolve from subcultures, they can also emerge from white supremacist social scenes. White supremacists often arrange formal or informal social gatherings of like-minded people in a particular geographic area, such as a "meet up" of white supremacists that might revolve around a barbecue. Some may socialize on a regular basis with other white supremacists in an area, like some of the Daily Stormer-associated "book clubs" that have recently appeared around the country. These social situations can occasionally prompt friends or acquaintances to decide to go to the "next level" and actually form a more formal group. In rare circumstances, members of a particular white supremacist family may form the nucleus of such a group rather than evolving from a social circle.

6. Copycats

Copycatting occurs when people seek to replicate a particular type of extremist group in their own location. This is not simply a case of an existing extremist group expanding into new geographic areas, though the distinctions may blur if the extremist group is highly decentralized.

Copycatting is most common within new extremist movements and is a significant way such movements spread. Because the white supremacist movement is an old and established movement, it offers fewer opportunities for large-scale copycatting than some other extremist movements have, but the process can occasionally occur, particularly when a new variation of white supremacy or a new type of group emerges.

Perhaps the best example of this phenomenon occurred in the 1980s with the nationwide proliferation of white supremacist prison gangs. For many years, the Aryan Brotherhood (based in the California and federal prison systems) was the only major white supremacist prison gang, but as various prison systems desegregated in the 80s, inmates copied the idea of the Aryan Brotherhood in their own state prison systems, often even stealing the name: Aryan Brotherhood of Texas, Ohio Aryan Brotherhood, Arizona Aryan Brotherhood, and so forth. These gangs were not chapters or subgroups of the original Aryan Brotherhood but rather independent and unrelated copies of it.

Copycatting can also occur on a smaller scale within the white supremacist movement, such as the so-called "white student unions" that some young white supremacists have attempted to establish at universities. Most of these groups, however, were very short-lived.

7. Social Media Groups

In recent years, a number of new extremist groups have emerged from social media. For example, extremists may create a Facebook "group" that eventually takes on a life of its own and evolves into an actual "in real life" group. Thanks to the speed and reach of social media, groups organizing by this method can spread quite quickly.

In early 2016, for example, the Soldiers of Odin USA formed using Facebook, bringing together white supremacists, anti-government extremists and anti-immigration extremists to oppose immigration and refugees. Within just a couple of months, thousands of people had expressed support for or affiliation with the Soldiers of Odin and chapters had formed in most states. However, like many groups that form on social media, members were spread widely but thinly and the number of people actually committed to the group turned out to be considerably fewer than suggested by its Facebook statistics.

8. Mutations

Some extremist groups don't form as extremist groups—they form as some other sort of organization but mutate over time into something more extreme. The most famous example of this type of group formation is the original Ku Klux Klan, which was formed as a social club in the mid-1860s by a small group of friends and Confederate veterans in Tennessee. It quickly evolved into something far more sinister, and within short order it became a violent terrorist movement that threatened Reconstruction state governments in the South.

In some cases, a mutation is contingent on a dominant or charismatic personality. In the 2000s, the Michigan State University chapter of the conservative college group Young Americans for Freedom became so radicalized under the leadership of Kyle Bristow that the chapter essentially became a hate group. Bristow eventually resigned from the group, going his own way as a white supremacist, and in 2016 founded his own hate group, the so-called "Foundation for the Marketplace of Ideas."

The Trump Administration's Tolerance of White Supremacists Has Led to Violent Anti-Semitism

Aaron Keyak

Aaron Keyak is the former head of the National Jewish Democratic Council and co-founder of Bluelight Strategies, a Washington, DC-based communications firm.

Oct. 27 marked the one-year anniversary of the horrific shooting at the Tree of Life synagogue in Pittsburgh. A lone gunman, armed with an AR-15, entered the sanctuary shouting anti-Semitic slurs, killing 11 congregants and injuring many others. The incident marked the deadliest assault on the Jewish community in the history of America.

Unfortunately, this act did not occur in isolation. Anti-Semitism is not only alive and dangerous in the United States, but it is on the rise.

On Oct. 12, a Jewish man in the Crown Heights neighborhood of New York was slapped across the face and called "a dirty Jew"—the latest in a growing series of violent assaults targeting Jews around Brooklyn.

Also in October, anti-Semitic posters were plastered to the doors of a synagogue in Grand Rapids, Michigan, featuring the head of Hitler with the caption "Did you forget about me?" and the slogan that it's time for a "crusade against Semite-led subhumans." (Additionally, *J.* [the Jewish News of Northern California] recently reported on anti-Semitic hate flyers that were posted at a Modesto church; see tinyurl.com/jweekly-modestohate.)

In a just-released survey by the American Jewish Committee, more than 80 percent of Jewish respondents say they have witnessed an increase in anti-Semitic incidents in the United States over the

"Anti-Semitism Is Rising in the US—and Many Jews Blame Trump," by Aaron Keyak, The Jewish News of Northern California, October 28, 2019. Reprinted by permission.

past five years, with 43 percent indicating that the increase has been significant.

That anti-Semitism is spiking is not only a matter of perception, however. The Anti-Defamation League reported a 150 percent increase in recorded incidents comparing 2013 with 2018.

American Jews clearly see that the hike in white supremacy goes hand in hand with the hike in anti-Semitic incidents across our country: 89 percent of AJC respondents believe the extreme political right presents a threat to Jews.

Donald Trump's presidency has helped embolden white supremacy throughout America. He has routinely refused to condemn their hatred. At the same time as Trump often refuses to criticize far-right extremist groups, he himself has engaged in harmful rhetoric, claiming in August that any Jewish person who votes for a Democrat shows "either a total lack of knowledge or great disloyalty." Throughout history, we know how deadly questions of Jewish loyalty can be.

It is no wonder that the AJC poll showed nearly three-quarters of Jewish voters disapprove of Trump's handling of the anti-Semitism threat, with more than six in 10 showing strong disapproval. Only 22 percent of Jewish voters have a favorable opinion of Trump's performance; 76 percent have an unfavorable opinion.

Forty-one percent of respondents to AJC's survey believe that the Republican Party bears all or close to all responsibility for the current levels of anti-Semitism. And 58 percent stated that the Democratic Party bears no, or close to no, responsibility for it.

It's therefore hardly surprising that American Jews continue to show strong support for the Democratic Party; in the 2018 midterm elections, exit polls showed that three-quarters of Jewish Americans voted for Democrats. Despite what President Trump falsely claims, the Democratic Party remains our political home.

Now, Jews are speaking out. Anti-Semitism is an existential threat to our community and we all have a role to play to stop it. The impact is felt communally as well as individually, from increased security patrols to mentally scoping out the best exit from your shul seat for yourself and your children if, God forbid, the worst were to happen. Tragically it is not a matter of whether another terrorist attack will occur, it is a matter of when.

What's more: This cannot be a partisan fight. Democrats must do more to call out anti-Semitism on the far left, while Republicans must stand up against Jew-hatred on the right.

When 82 percent of US Jews view the boycott, divestment and sanctions movement's delegitimization of Israel as fundamentally anti-Semitic, those progressives, sadly including a couple of members of Congress, who still support this form of "protest" should listen. Unwittingly or not, they are cozying up to those who want the world's only Jewish state to cease to exist.

At the same time, Trump's own rhetoric, equating civil rights protesters and neo-Nazis at Charlottesville's Unite the Right rally as "very fine people, on both sides" emboldens the violent Jew-haters who look up to him.

That is only one example of the countless times that the occupant of the most powerful elected office on Earth has failed to stand up to racists and anti-Semites. His supporters in our own community must consider how to do much more to challenge this.

As we honor those who were murdered a year ago at the Tree of Life synagogue, we must stand united against hate and redouble our efforts to fight anti-Semitism—wherever it is found, and not least among those who claim to be our political brethren.

Mass Shootings Are One Threat of Extremism

Anti-Defamation League

The Anti-Defamation League (ADL) is an international non-governmental organization based in the US. It works to oppose extremism and anti-Semitism.

The issue of gun violence and mass shootings is in the news frequently. Young people are usually aware of what is happening and will want to talk about it. However, it is a sensitive, scary, and potentially painful topic. Before raising the matter with children, consider your child's personality. Will the conversation ease your child's fears or add to it?

For some youth, it is better to be proactive and raise the topic without their prompting. For others, following their lead and their questions is a better approach. When you discuss this topic with children, here are some things to keep in mind:

- Be prepared yourself so you can be there for them emotionally. Make sure you have set aside enough time to hear children's thoughts, questions, and feelings.
- Provide accurate information about their school's safety procedures and reassure them that they are safe.
- Be careful when describing the perpetrator. Do not stereotype and make assumptions about the person. Mental health is an example. One in four adults experience mental health issues annually. The majority of people with these issues are not violent.
- Emphasize the helpers, including those who took care of and helped the victims. It is helpful to convey to children your concern and compassion. You can then think together with them about something you can do to help.

"Gun Violence and Mass Shootings," Anti-Defamation League. Published with permission of the Anti-Defamation League, New York, NY. All rights reserved.

Mass Shootings and Their Impact: El Paso, Texas

On August 3, 2019, an active shooter opened fire at a Walmart store in a shopping center in El Paso, Texas. Twenty-two people were killed, and dozens were injured. This shooting is considered one of the deadliest in the history of Texas. Law enforcement confirmed the shooter wrote a four-page manifesto that embraces white supremacist and anti-immigrant views. Police disclosed that the suspect admitted he was targeting Mexican people.

Another Shooting in Dayton, Ohio

Less than 24 hours after the El Paso murder, another deadly shooting took place outside a bar in Dayton, Ohio. At least nine people were killed and sixteen people were injured. The alleged gunman was shot dead by the police.

Tree of Life Synagogue Shooting

On October 27, 2018, a gunman, identified as Robert Bowers, armed with an assault rifle and several handguns, entered the Tree of Life synagogue in Pittsburgh, PA, and yelled, "All Jews Must Die" as he opened fire. Described as the deadliest attack against the Jewish community in the US, eleven congregants were killed; four police officers and two others were wounded.

Shooting at Marjory Stoneman Douglas HS in Parkland, Florida

On February 14, 2018, seventeen people—including students and adults—were killed in a shooting at Marjory Stoneman Douglas High School in Parkland, Florida. The gunman, Nikolas Cruz, was a nineteen-year-old former student of the school. Authorities reported that he was armed with a semiautomatic assault rifle and countless magazines. People were killed both inside and outside the school. The Parkland shooting is among the ten deadliest mass shootings in modern US history.

Other Mass Shootings

In recent years, there have been a variety of mass shootings. On October 1, 2017, a gunman at a Las Vegas hotel fired a barrage of gunfire into a crowd of concertgoers at the Route 91 Harvest Festival, resulting in the killing of 59 people and injuring hundreds of others.

On June 12, 2016, a gunman named Omar Mateen, an American-born man, pledged his allegiance to ISIS. He then went into a gay nightclub in Orlando, FL, and shot and killed 49 people and injured 53 others.

On December 2, 2015, two assailants opened fire at a center for people with disabilities in San Bernardino, California; 14 people were killed and 21 others were wounded.

That deadly mass shooting came on the heels of another tragic event on November 27, 2015, in which Robert Lewis Dear embarked upon a deadly shooting spree at a Planned Parenthood clinic. Two people and a police officer were killed and nine others were wounded.

On October 1, 2015, a mass shooting at Umpqua Community College in Oregon left nine students dead and another nine injured. The gunman, Christopher Harper-Mercer, killed himself after an exchange of gunfire with the police.

What Can Be Done About Gun Violence?

Mass shootings often raise a lot of feelings that range from sadness and heartbreak to anger and frustration. They also usually lead to a public conversation about gun laws and what our government can and should do. In 2012 after the mass shooting of twenty young children and six adults at Sandy Hook Elementary School in Newtown, CT, President Obama proposed legislation to overhaul gun laws. The proposals included universal background checks, new and expanded assault weapon and high-capacity magazine bans and other measures to prevent mass shootings. Several months later, it failed to pass the Senate.

What Are Mass Shootings?

Understanding mass shootings, typically defined as the murder of four or more people, school shootings and other gun-related deaths, is complex. According to a Congressional Research Service in 2013, there had been 78 mass murders carried out with guns during the thirty-year period of 1982-2012. Because there is not one standard way to tally the number of mass school shootings, in the period between 2000 and 2013, the FBI identified 160 active shooter incidents, where one or more shooters were actively engaged in killing or attempted killing in a confined and populated location. It used this definition to describe instances like Sandy Hook or the Virginia Tech shooting in 2007. Since 2011, the rate of mass shootings has tripled.

The Second Amendment

Defenders of gun rights say that proposed gun regulations violate the Second Amendment. The second amendment states: "A well-regulated Militia, being necessary to the security of a free State, the right of the people to keep and bear Arms, shall not be infringed." After the Newtown shooting, the president of the National Rifle Association (NRA), a national nonprofit organization that advocates and lobbies for gun rights, spoke about the incident. He said, "The only thing that stops a bad guy with a gun is a good guy with a gun." Indeed, many people believe that guns prevent crime from happening.

Gun Violence in the US

In addition to mass shootings, there are other relevant numbers about gun violence in the states. More than 32,000 people per year are killed by guns—which translates to approximately 88 gun deaths per day. Compared to peer nations, including Germany, England and Canada, people are much more likely to die from guns in the US than in other countries.

According to the Pew Research Center's 2017 public opinion poll on gun proposals, the percentage of the public who agree that we should:

- Prevent people who are mentally ill from purchasing guns: 89%
- Implement background checks for private sales and gun shows: 84%
- Bar gun purchases by people on no-fly or watch lists: 83%
- Create a federal database to track gun sales: 71%
- Ban assault-style weapons: 68%
- Ban high-capacity magazines: 65%

When mass shootings occur, people frequently search for the reason and often mental illness is cited as the culprit. It is much more complicated than that; it is difficult to come up with one reason or risk factor. There are usually a multitude of reasons for these shootings, including but not limited to: domestic terrorism, availability of guns, romanticism with violence and multiple risk factors operating simultaneously (e.g., depression, narcissism, alienation, lack of trust, poor coping skills, fascination with violence-filled entertainment, revenge fantasies, attempted suicide attempts in the past, etc.).

Questions to Start the Conversation

- How do you feel about what you know and have heard about gun violence and mass shootings? What else do you want to know?
- Do you know people who have different opinions on gun violence? What do they say and how does this influence (or not) your point of view?
- What do you think should be done to keep people safe from gun violence?
- Why do you think so many people feel it is important to protect people's right to own guns?

- Why do you think there are so many more mass shootings than there used to be?

Questions to Dig Deeper

- What can we do "to get our government to do something about gun violence" as President Obama urged after the 2015 school shooting in Oregon?
- How is the NRA successful in making their case that guns should not be regulated more than they already are?
- Why do you think that Congress has not been able to pass the legislation to try to prevent mass shootings?

Ideas for Taking Action

Ask: What can we do to help? What actions might make a difference?

- Write a letter to your members of Congress (or to the school or local newspaper) that conveys your position about gun violence and what you think should be done about it.
- Educate others about this topic by sharing information on social media, engaging in personal conversations or organizing an educational forum or debate in school.
- Join with or hold a fundraiser to support gun violence prevention advocacy organizations such as Newtown Action Alliance, Brady Campaign to Prevent Gun Violence, Everytown for Gun Safety and Moms Demand.

Far-Right Hate Groups Are a Threat to Democratic Society

Southern Poverty Law Center

The Southern Poverty Law Center (SPLC) is an American nonprofit legal advocacy organization that focuses on civil rights and public interest law.

The [Southern Poverty Law Center keeps] a detailed listing of major terrorist plots and racist rampages that have emerged from the American radical right in the years since the 1995 Oklahoma City bombing. These have included plans to bomb government buildings, banks, refineries, utilities, clinics, synagogues, mosques, memorials and bridges; to assassinate police officers, judges, politicians, civil rights figures and others; to rob banks, armored cars and other criminals; and to amass illegal machine guns, missiles, explosives and biological and chemical weapons. Most contemplated the deaths of large numbers of people—in one case, as many as 30,000, or 10 times the number murdered on Sept. 11, 2001.

Here are the stories of plots, conspiracies and racist rampages [in 2019 alone]—plots and violence waged against a democratic America.

August 9, 2019

Agents with the Florida Department of Law Enforcement (FDLE) arrested Richard Dean Clayton, 26, of Winter Park for allegedly threatening to attack a Walmart a day after a mass shooter in El Paso left 22 dead and more than two dozen injured at a Walmart store there. The FDLE, in a press release, said it began its investigation Aug. 6 after Clayton allegedly made a threat on Facebook saying that "3 more days of probation left" and then he would get his AR-15 rifle back. The post read, "Don't go to Walmart next week," the

"Terror from the Right," Southern Poverty Law Center. Reprinted by permission.

FDLE stated. Investigators say that Clayton appears to believe in white supremacist ideology and has a history of posting threats and racist and antisemitic comments on Facebook using fake accounts, including an image of a swastika and references to an ethnostate. The *Orlando Sentinel*, citing a police report, said Clayton asked one of the officers if he was Hispanic, saying: "They are what is wrong with this country. They come in and are ruining everything." Clayton is charged with making written threats to kill or do bodily harm. He appeared in court Aug. 10 and his bail was lowered from $25,000 to $15,000 on the condition he stay 1,000 feet away from any Walmart store.

August 8, 2019

Conor Climo, 23, is charged in federal court in Nevada with one count of possession of an unregistered firearm—the components of a destructive device. Authorities arrested Climo in Las Vegas, Nevada, following a FBI-led Joint Terrorism Task Force investigation.

The Department of Justice, in a press release, alleges that Climo used encrypted online methods to communicate with white supremacists. NBC News, citing FBI sources, alleged the suspect also communicated with members of the neo-Nazi group Atomwaffen Division.

The DOJ alleges Climo used encrypted messages to chat online about attacking a Las Vegas synagogue and making Molotov cocktails and improvised explosive devices. The DOJ claims Climo tried to recruit a homeless person to conduct surveillance on a synagogue and wanted to target patrons of an LGBTQ bar in downtown Las Vegas. Investigators, according to the *New York Times*, found sketched images in Climo's home portraying timed-explosive devices and infantry squads attacking the bar with guns. Climo faces a maximum penalty of 10 years in prison and a $250,000 fine.

August 7, 2019

Justin Olsen, 18, of Boardman, Ohio, was arrested and later charged with making threats against law enforcement. An investigation. according to authorities, revealed his online support of mass shootings. Olsen lived in his father's house in which authorities say they found 25 guns, including AR-15 style rifles and semi-automatic pistols, and 10,000 rounds of ammunition. According to an affidavit, Olsen, who had been under investigation since February, used the handle "ArmyofChrist" on iFunny, a website where users post on a variety of topics. Olsen, according to the affidavit, told fellow users that he supported mass shootings and attacks on Planned Parenthood. The affidavit claims Olsen called for shooting "every federal agent on site" following a June discussion about the 1993 Branch Davidian standoff in Waco, Texas. Olsen, authorities say, admitted that he posted comments about violence on iFunny, but said they were "only a joke." He remains in the Mahoning County Jail without bond.

August 3, 2019

A man opened fire with an AK-47 style assault rifle just after 11 a.m. local time in an El Paso, Texas, Walmart, killing 22 and injuring 26. Parents and children were taking advantage of a tax-free shopping day before the beginning of school. El Paso is nearly 80% Hispanic and is located just across the US-Mexico border from Ciudad Juarez. Law enforcement arrested a suspect, Patrick Crusius, 21, of Allen, Texas. Authorities believe the suspect may also be the author of a racist, anti-immigrant document that was posted to the site 8chan just before the shooting. The document's author expresses white nationalist talking points about "ethnic displacement," expresses displeasure at "race-mixing," and refers to the attack as a response to the "Hispanic invasion of Texas." The author also mentions the suspect in the Christchurch, New Zealand, mass shooting in March at two mosques in which 51 people died. Officials are pursuing capital murder charges against the suspect, and federal authorities are treating the El Paso mass shooting as a case of domestic terrorism. The Justice Department is also considering bringing federal hate crime and federal firearm charges, which carry a possible death penalty.

April 27, 2019

One person was killed and three were injured when a gunman entered the Chabad synagogue in Poway, California, and opened fire with an AR-15 style weapon. The attack came exactly six months after the Pittsburgh synagogue shooting that left 11 dead. An federal affidavit claims the suspect in the California shooting, John T. Earnest, 19, said the "Jewish people are destroying the white race."

The suspect fled the building after his gun apparently jammed. The suspect later called the California Highway Patrol and reported his location on Interstate 15 in Rancho Bernardo and then surrendered to a police officer who was responding to the attack. Around the time of the shooting, officials found an antisemitic document posted to online message board 8chan that was filled with racist slurs and white nationalist conspiracy theories. The author, writing under the name John Earnest, claims in the document to have been inspired by a New Zealand mosque shooting that killed 51 people and claims responsibility for a mosque fire in Escondido, California, in March. Earnest was charged with one count of murder with a hate crime special circumstances and gun allegations and one count of arson of a house of worship. He was later indicted by a federal grand jury and faces 113 federal counts, including hate crimes.

February 14, 2019

The FBI arrested US Coast Guard Lt. Christopher Hasson of Silver Spring, Maryland, after labeling him a domestic terrorist who pushed for a "white homeland" and had a hit list of Democratic politicians and media figures.

Hasson had been based at Coast Guard headquarters in Washington, DC. The FBI says Hasson self-identified as a white nationalist and was an admirer of Norwegian domestic terrorist Anders Breivik, who killed 77 people in a rampage over Muslim immigration. He also searched online for pro-Russian, neo-fascist and neo-Nazi literature.

Hasson stockpiled weapons and more than 1,000 rounds of ammunition, the FBI said, at his Maryland home.

Among the targets Hasson listed were US Senators Cory Booker, Elizabeth Warren, Kamala Harris and Richard Blumenthal, former Vice President Joe Biden and MSNBC hosts Ari Melber, Chris Hayes and Joe Scarborough.

Hasson also wrote to a longtime neo-Nazi about the idea of "focused violence."

"I never saw a reason for mass protest or wearing uniforms marching around provoking people with swastikas etc.," Hasson wrote. "I was and am a man of action you cannot change minds protesting like that."

Hasson was charged with drug and weapons offenses in Maryland.

The Police Label Protesters "Extremists" to Justify Intense Surveillance

Kevin Blowe

Kevin Blowe is the coordinator of the Network for Police Monitoring (Netpol), a UK-based organization that monitors protest and street policing in order to challenge excessive policing that threatens civil rights.

P riti Patel probably thought she was helping when she tried to defend counter-terrorism police from the condemnation that followed last week's story in the *Guardian* revealing the inclusion of Extinction Rebellion (XR) in a guide on supposed "extreme or violent ideologies."

The document has apparently now been withdrawn. Nevertheless, the home secretary's insistence that the police always make decisions based on the "risk to the public, security risks, security threats" does inevitably lead to an obvious, unanswered question. If she is right, how exactly did Counter Terrorism Policing South East (CTPSE), which wrote and published the guide, manage to make what even it admits was a significant "error of judgment"?

The answer lies in how alleged risks posed by protest groups are assessed. To begin with, it may surprise many that there is no legal definition of what "domestic extremism" even means, leaving the police with complete discretion in deciding what it covers. "Extremism" and "domestic extremism" are used interchangeably by the police to differentiate from terrorism. The current criteria is so broad and ambiguous that David Anderson, a former independent reviewer of terrorism legislation, has described it as "manifestly deficient," and last summer, the Home Office finally confirmed it had stopped using such terms. The police, as we have seen, have not.

In practice, decisions about who is labelled an "extremist" are made in secret by police units concerned more about their ideas of security and defending public order than about human rights and by officers who are often deeply antagonistic towards protesters challenging the corporate and political orthodoxies of the day.

The full extent of such hostility was set out in a Policy Exchange report on XR co-authored last year by Richard Walton, the former head of the Metropolitan police's counter-terrorism command. Walton claimed, extraordinarily, that what he saw as "the underlying extremism of the campaign" had been "largely obscured from public view by what many see as the fundamental legitimacy of their stated cause."

It is hardly surprising, therefore, that assessments of alleged "risk" are never neutral. Invariably, as the CTPSE guide claimed, just having an "anti-establishment philosophy," taking part in entirely non-violent direct action and even participation in "planned school walkouts" is enough for the police to classify individual campaigners as a threat.

In turn, this classification provides police with the justification for intensive surveillance, which can be extremely intrusive and intimidating.

XR is far from the first environmental campaign to receive this kind of police attention. More than a decade ago the anti-aviation group Plane Stupid was targeted and it is nine years since Mark Kennedy was exposed as an undercover police officer who infiltrated annual climate camp gatherings.

However, the most recent targets have been opponents of fracking, with sustained surveillance from regional counter-terrorism units. Netpol, the organisation I run to monitor public order, protest and street policing, has documented the experiences of the anti-fracking movement for five years and these provide an important reminder of why no matter what promises are made now, there are no guarantees the police will stop categorising XR as "extremists" in the future.

In December 2016, negative media coverage forced the Home Office to declare that "support for anti-fracking is not an indicator of vulnerability" to extremism. This followed reports about City of York council and a school in North Yorkshire including anti-fracking campaigns in their Prevent counter-terrorism advice. However, months later, leaked "counter-terrorism local profiles"— again the work of the regional police unit in the south-east of England—identified protests in Sussex as a "priority theme ... where increased tensions or vulnerabilities may exist."

As recently as October 2019, there was evidence of Surrey county council claiming local police had advised it that anti-fracking activities were among their "main extremist areas of concern" (alongside the far right) and that any protest, no matter how peaceful, was "extremist."

It is clear that once the current controversy dies down, it will be only a matter of time before XR and other climate activists are again labelled as an "extremist risk." The group has indicated it may bring legal action to have its name removed from any list but perhaps XR would be better served by putting its weight behind the call for the complete abolition of the "domestic extremist" label for everyone.

To protect freedom to protest, the government also needs to completely separate secretive counter-terrorism units from the policing of non-violent protests. They have no business involving themselves in legitimate political activity.

Until this happens, it seems unlikely anyone will ever be held to account for "errors of judgment," no matter how potentially damaging the consequences are for those labelled a safeguarding risk. Officers will simply carry on, as they have for decades, trying to find imagined threats in any new and emerging protest movement and then spying on and disrupting their campaigns. It's time this finally stopped for good.

It Is Unrealistic to Expect an Organization to Objectively Scrutinize Hate Groups

Robby Soave

Robby Soave is a senior editor at Reason *magazine. He also serves on the DC Advisory Committee to the US Commission on Civil Rights.*

Controversy has struck the Southern Poverty Law Center, the formidable progressive law firm best known for tracking hate groups in the US. Co-founder Morris Dees, President Richard Cohen, and other top executives are exiting the organization amidst a staff uprising over alleged sexual and racial harassment in the work place.

The leadership shakeup, fueled by allegations that black staffers were shut out of key positions and that Dees personally harassed female staffers, has brought the SPLC considerable media scrutiny, and it's about time. Regardless of whether these specific accusations have merit, the SPLC should face a reckoning over its extremely shoddy work, which has mistakenly promoted the idea that fringe hate groups are a rising threat.

Peddling this false narrative has long been the SPLC's business model, and the Trump years have been especially profitable, since the group was almost perfectly positioned to capitalize on growing liberal fears about hate crimes, resurgent white nationalism, and the alt-right. Over the course of the Trump campaign and presidency, the SPLC has added dozens of staffers, saw its social media following rise dramatically, ramped up its fundraising, and built a $200 million endowment. Its role has been to provide intellectual support for a central narrative of the #Resistance: Hate, broadly defined, is surging across America, and Trump is to blame.

"The Southern Poverty Law Center Is Both a Terrible Place to Work and a Place That Does Terrible Work," by Robby Soave, Reason.com and *Reason* magazine, March 27, 2019. Reprinted by permission.

But the SPLC's hate tally is incredibly suspect, as leftist writer Nathan Robinson explained in a terrific article for *Current Affairs*. According to the SPLC's hate map, there were more than 1,000 hate groups in the US in 2018—nearly twice as many as existed in 2000. The number has increased every year since 2014.

The map is littered with dots that provide more information on each specific group, and this is where the SPLC gives away the game. Consider a random state—Oklahoma, for example, is home to nine distinct hate groups, by the SPLC's count. Five of them, though, are black nationalist groups: the Nation of Islam, Israel United in Christ, etc. The SPLC counts each chapter of these groups separately, so the Nation of Islam counts as two separate hate groups within Oklahoma (its various chapters in other states are also tallied separately). The map makes no attempt to contextualize all of this—no information is given on the relative size or influence of each group.

In his piece, Robinson describes the map as an "outright fraud," and it's hard to argue with him:

> In fact, when you actually look at the hate map, you find something interesting: Many of these "groups" barely seem to exist at all. A "Holocaust denial" group in Kerrville, Texas, called "carolynyeager.net" appears to just be a woman called Carolyn Yeager. A "male supremacy" group called Return of Kings is apparently just a blog published by pick-up artist Roosh V and a couple of his friends, and the most recent post is an announcement from six months ago that the project was on indefinite hiatus. Tony Alamo, the abusive cult leader of "Tony Alamo Christian Ministries," died in prison in 2017. (Though his ministry's website still promotes "Tony Alamo's Unreleased Beatles Album.") A "black nationalist" group in Atlanta called "Luxor Couture" appears to be an African fashion boutique. "Sharkhunters International" is one guy who really likes U-boats and takes small groups of sad Nazis on tours to see ruins and relics. And good luck finding out much about the "Samanta Roy Institute of Science and Technology," which—if it is currently

operative at all—is a tiny anti-Catholic cult based in Shawano, Wisconsin.

Sloppily tallying hate in service of a greater narrative is par for the course at the SPLC. The group's report on Trump-inspired schoolyard bullying is similarly flawed: Its survey was unscientific, and based on anecdotes reported by members of the SPLC's mailing list.

When it comes to misleading hate crime data, the SPLC is far from the only offender. Many in the media have exaggerated a finding by the Anti-Defamation League that anti-Semitic hate has increased 57 percent under Trump. (Bomb threats made by an Israeli teenager were largely responsible for the perceived increase: anti-Semitic assaults actually decreased substantially.) The FBI's hate crime data has also been widely mischaracterized.

Still, the SPLC stands out. It previously characterized Maajid Nawaz as an anti-Muslim extremist—but Nawaz is a progressive whose work is aimed at de-radicalizing Muslim extremists. To this day, the SPLC lists Charles Murray's ideology as "white nationalist."

Over at *National Review*, David French urges the SPLC to "rediscover its roots." The organization used to do much more work aligned with its name: representing impoverished death row inmates, for example, and battling the KKK in court. It has plenty of money and could hire an army of lawyers to really make a difference in the lives of criminal defendants. But first, the organization needs to give up on the project of inflating the threat posed by fringe nutcases.

CHAPTER 3

Is Extremist Expression Dangerous in Itself?

Overview: Extremist Disinformation Is Used to Impact Politics and Society

Dean Jackson

Dean Jackson is an assistant program officer with the National Endowment for Democracy's internal think tank, the International Forum for Democracy.

Disinformation—the use of half-truth and non-rational argument to manipulate public opinion in pursuit of political objectives—is a growing threat to the public sphere in countries around the world. The challenge posed by Russian disinformation has attracted significant attention in the United States and Europe; over time, observers have noted its role in "hybrid warfare," its use to degrade public trust in media and state institutions, and its ability to amplify social division, resentment, and fear.

But Moscow is merely the most prominent purveyor of disinformation, not its sole source. Political actors around the world, ranging in size from state agencies to individuals, have found ways to exploit the economics of digital advertising and the fast-paced nature of the modern information ecosystem for their political advantage. Growing appreciation of the problem's scale invites a shift in frame: from national security threat from a discrete actor to a broader appreciation of political-economic weaknesses in the contemporary information space.

Disinformation has a wider variety of purposes, in a wider variety of settings, than is commonly appreciated. In the short term, it can be used to distract from an issue, obscure the truth, or to inspire its consumers to take a certain course of action. In the long-term, disinformation can be part of a strategy to shape the information environment in which individuals, governments, and other actors form beliefs and make decisions.

"Issue Brief: How Disinformation Impacts Politics and Publics," by Dean Jackson, National Endowment for Democracy, May 29, 2018. Reprinted by permission.

Disinformation as a Reactive Tactic

In the short term, disinformation can be utilized reactively by different entities: for example, when Russian-backed fighters in Eastern Ukraine shot down a commercial airliner, Russian state media went into overdrive proposing multiple, often conflicting alternative explanations for the plane's crash.

Disinformation's applications have also been evident in Syria, where Russian diplomats, media, and intelligence services have falsified evidence, pushed misleading narratives, and spread falsehoods relating to the role of Russia's airstrikes, as well as to obscure evidence of the Syrian government's use of chemical weapons.

Another common technique is to react to a crisis by flooding the information space and drowning out discussion. After opposition protests broke out in Syria during 2011, newly-created Twitter accounts began harassing Syrian users, and social media researches allege that the Assad regime paid a public relations firm to flood opposition hashtags with photos of nature scenery and sports scores.

Bots and Trolls Shape Political Conversation Online

Online trolling, harassment, and distraction—especially by highly active automated accounts—are a key component of the modern disinformation purveyor's toolkit. These techniques push independent voices out of public spaces and are sometimes considered a new form of political censorship. The Chinese Communist Party (CCP) was an early pioneer of this approach: for at least a decade, Beijing has deployed a "fifty-cent party" (apocryphally named for posters' going rate per post) to "astroturf" support for the government and derail online political conversations that could spark mass mobilization. Recent estimates suggest this effort encompasses two million individuals, many of them state employees, and produces nearly 450 million social media posts per year.

Over time, similar approaches became a common aspect of authoritarian information manipulation and were later amplified through automation. In the early to mid-2000s, the Russian government began recruiting human commenters before later adopting the use of automated "bot" accounts. One study suggests that on Twitter more than half of tweets in Russian are produced by automated accounts. Aiming to avoid detection, many disinformation campaigns now avail themselves of accounts that are partially automated, partially controlled by human users; these are often referred to as cyborg or sock puppet accounts.

In recent years, the use of bots and trolls to shape online discussion has become so common across countries that it could be considered a widely exploited bug in the digital public square extending far beyond conflict or authoritarian settings. In Mexico, paid political consultants orchestrated the theft of campaign secrets and the large scale distribution of disinformation to voters. Such activity continues to this day, as pro-government accounts swarm political hashtags, threaten the lives of activists, and marginalize protesters.

In the Philippines, where the public square faces significant threats both online and off, interview-based research has explored a sophisticated "underground" public relations industry in which digital strategists, social media influencers, and paid commenters compete to deliver their clients the greatest degree of control over political narratives on the internet. In a stroke of market innovation, the subcontracting of digital disinformation in the Philippines has tied the financial and career incentives of competing freelancers to the objectives of national political parties, to devastating effect.

Proactive Disinformation and the "Demand Side" of the Challenge

The effectiveness of "reactive" disinformation is limited by the unpredictability of real-world events. While it can offer those who use it a lifeline in times of crisis, reactive disinformation is by definition a response to unexpected, uncontrollable, or undesirable events and therefore generally used by those in disadvantageous strategic positions. Used proactively, disinformation provides much greater potential to move audiences to action, shape or confuse public understanding, and influence political events.

However, it does not provide a blank canvas on which to work. Effective disinformation campaigns usually draw on preexisting divides within target societies and produce content for which there is societal demand. Disinformation is at its most dangerous when amplifying existing political beliefs and divisions as opposed to introducing new beliefs or narratives into the public sphere. It is effective in doing so in part due to low trust in media and in part due to cognitive biases that make many consumers more likely to believe content that confirms their beliefs, to prefer partisan cheerleading over the conclusions of fact-checkers, and to share content that makes them angry or afraid. Research into the impact of social media use on political polarization is ongoing, but at a minimum suggests that the emergence of social media platforms as news sources has diminished the power of traditional "gatekeepers" of news and information. In turn, social media seems to have increased the social and political influence of a voracious subset of news consumers engaged in "motivated reasoning"—the selected interpretation of information to justify one's preexisting beliefs, stances, or desires. These factors, combined with the speed at which information spreads online, create ideal conditions for disinformation campaigns.

Digital Disinformation Can Inspire Real-World Action

Proactive disinformation campaigns can achieve real-world impact by influencing the actions of its consumers. A prominent example comes from Germany's 2016 "Lisa case," which ignited nationwide debate over the country's resettlement of Middle Eastern refugees and offered Moscow an opportunity to stoke divisions within Germany. Lisa, a thirteen year-old Russian-German girl, alleged that two migrant men kidnapped and raped her; the allegations were later proven to be untrue, but not before Russian state media actively spread the story and the Russian Foreign Minister publicly accused Berlin of a cover up. In Germany, thousands protested the government's handling of the case. By using media and diplomatic resources to promote a false story at a time of rising German anti-migrant sentiment, Moscow sought to exploit domestic German political divides to encourage mass demonstrations and damage the German government politically.

Digital disinformation often promotes xenophobic sentiment, and hate speech is common. In India, far-right religious figures used messaging applications to spread false claims about religious minorities, sparking communal violence. In Indonesia, political and religious leaders have decried the spread of hate speech and rumors over social media, which played a pivotal role in the Jakarta mayoral election.

Mass media have been used to spread disinformation and hate speech in the past, and have played a key role in modern genocides. Social media is now playing a similar role in contemporary atrocities: in Burma, for instance, ultranationalist Buddhist monks have used social media to mobilize supporters and instigate violence against the Rohingya, a persecuted Muslim minority group.

Disinformation During Elections

Often, disinformation aims to influence citizens' decisions to vote (or to abstain from voting). The use of disinformation around elections is probably only slightly younger than representative democracy itself, but the reach, speed, and low cost of disseminating disinformation over social media has amplified this problem.

The actors involved are often subnational political figures or organizations, although state organs are sometimes complicit. In South Korea, for example, the role of state-spread disinformation during the country's 2012 presidential election was exposed after an investigation found that the National Intelligence Service generated more than 1.2 million Twitter messages supporting now-impeached

South Korean President Park Geun-hye (or, as is often the case with disinformation, denigrating her rival).

The 2017 Kenyan elections offer a valuable case study in the widespread use of domestically sourced disinformation in an electoral context. As in the Philippine case cited above, rival political factions created sophisticated digital operations, conscripting influential social media personalities, paid commentators, and armies of bot accounts. Digital advertising techniques amplified the spread of hate speech and disinformation targeting political opponents. Hoax websites imitating real news outlets produced disinformation at an industrial scale, with one study finding that nine in ten Kenyans had seen false information about the election online, and 87 percent of respondents believing that information to be deliberately false. These techniques—not unique to Kenya—proved dangerous at an exceptionally contentious political moment in a country where the previous elections led to bloodshed.

Foreign-Sourced Disinformation in Electoral Contexts

While disinformation frequently originates from domestic sources, some authoritarian governments increasingly use disinformation to influence elections beyond their borders. The Russian Federation stands out as the paramount example. Even a partial list of elections where Russian-produced or -supported disinformation has featured includes the French, German, and American elections in 2016 and 2017; the 2018 Czech presidential election; and the 2017 vote on Catalonian secession from Spain. In each of these cases, Moscow used a combination of state-owned international news outlets, smaller news sites linked to Moscow, and automated social media accounts, sometimes in tandem with leaks of stolen documents and communications.

It can be tremendously difficult to estimate the total effect of these simultaneous approaches, especially since international disinformation operations often imitate—or even promote—material produced by domestic actors. Sometimes, disinformation may flow the other way as it migrates from foreign sources to mainstream domestic news outlets.

Moscow is not the only actor in this space. While Beijing's international media strategy differs substantially from Moscow's, there is evidence it has experimented with disinformation in Taiwanese politics as part of a long-standing policy regarding unification between Taiwan and the People's Republic of China.

Disinformation as a Strategic Approach

Not every disinformation campaign is linked to a specific event such as an election. Disinformation can also be used to alter the broader information space in which people discuss issues, form beliefs, and make political decisions; it is sometimes deployed to promote a larger narrative over time or to degrade civic discourse by promoting division or cynicism.

Political actors have used disinformation for their benefit for millennia. However, the velocity and volume of disinformation in the contemporary information space seems to have amplified its effectiveness and left many members of the public increasingly angry, fearful, or disoriented. This, in turn, leaves publics even more vulnerable to future manipulation, resulting in a cycle of declining public trust in objective sources of information which some analysts call "truth decay."

Russian disinformation provides an instructive case study: at home and abroad, it draws on the principle that there is no such thing as objective truth. This allows Moscow to deploy multiple narratives and conspiracy theories when seeking to undermine public confidence in Western institutions, including claims that European politicians support Nazism in Ukraine, that the German government will pay for refugees and their "harems" to migrate to Europe, and that NATO planes spray mind-control chemicals over Poland. In addition to their explicit messages about Western wrongdoing, each of these stories implicitly suggests that Western media are concealing the truth from the public.

Consumers do not necessarily need to be persuaded by these stories—the introduction of doubt or anxiety may be enough to inspire distrust or political disengagement. In the case of the story about German taxpayers funding migrant harems, Moscow drew upon anti-migrant sentiment and resistance to German refugee policy to deepen political divides—not for the sake of inspiring immediate action, but because a divided and more fragile European Union serves Moscow's geopolitical interests.

As with many of the applications of disinformation described above, it remains a mistake to believe this approach is only or even primarily adopted by state actors; subnational political actors, business interests, and other parties also draw from these practices. An example comes from South Africa, where wealthy industrialists with close ties to South African politicians hired a British PR firm to distract from growing political corruption by inflaming race relations. By combining media outlets owned by the industrialists with a "wildly successful" social media campaign, the firm temporarily distracted from an ongoing process of state capture by manipulating social divides over racial inequality.

The disinformation challenge is about more than authoritarian propaganda or PR techniques. Longstanding vulnerabilities in human cognition, combined with new and emerging technology's impact on the information environment, allow for bad actors around the world to pursue political gains at the expense of democratic political discourse. The search for solutions must start by recognizing that the challenge is global and structural.

The Normalization of Extremist Rhetoric Has Caused an Increase in Hate Crimes

Naomi Elster

Dr. Naomi Elster has a PhD in breast cancer research. She is a nonfiction author who writes about science, health, and an evidence-based approach to women's issues.

In the first week following the election of a candidate endorsed by the Ku Klux Klan, 437 racist, sexist or xenophobic incidents took place, most of them against groups Trump had viciously denigrated during his campaign; people of color, women, LGBTQ people and immigrants. It's not unreasonable to suppose that the extreme rhetoric used in Trump's campaign may have incited at least some of those incidents. The night after the result was announced, I sat in a bar in Europe with an American friend who wondered aloud about going home for Christmas. "Is this result going to make all those extreme racists who've felt they had to be silent for years feel validated?" she asked. "To the point, they feel comfortable putting their hoods back on?"

My friend wouldn't have been comforted by the words of Richard Cohen, president of the Southern Poverty Law center. Quoted in the *New Yorker*, he said; "White supremacists are celebrating, and it's their time, the way they see it," referring to a survey of teachers which reported that more than half of them had seen an increase in hostile speech during the campaign, and that students of color have wondered aloud if their parents will be deported.

It can be far too easy for people not in risk groups to dismiss speech as empty words, or as something which is at worst, the kind of spiteful bullying any sensible person would ignore. But our right to safety must include psychological as well as physical safety, and a right not to feel threatened is fundamental to our very freedom.

Furthermore, the surge in hate incidents after the election wasn't limited to words. Civil liberties group the Anti-Defamation League reported a rise in vandalism and even physical attacks in the immediate aftermath of the election. The NYPD reported a huge spike in the incidence of and arrests for what they call "bias crimes," which increased 115 percent between the election and early December 2016, and Chief of Detectives Robert Boyce commented, "The national discourse has effects on hate crimes—hate speech I should say, hate speech." A Muslim transport worker was called a terrorist before being pushed down a flight of stairs, causing injury to her knee and ankle. A shove down stairs can be lethal. Although the Governor of New York did not make any reference to hate speech or the current climate when commenting on this attack on Facebook, he did stress that: "The work of the Hate Crimes Task Force has never been more urgent."

Freedom of speech is one thing. Hate speech is another.

Commonly defined as "speech that expresses or incites hatred toward people on the basis of some aspect of their identity"— hate speech is something that society must take seriously, not dismiss as something that might at worst hurt the feelings of some overly-sensitive liberals. There is evidence that hate speech predicts violence, that groups more exposed to hate speech are more likely to commit suicide, and that it causes what scientists call a "dehumanization effect" which makes it easier for us to justify suffering and harm caused to another human being. Influential civil rights organization The Southern Poverty Law Centre (SPLC) reports that there are 892 hate groups currently operating in the US, which seem to be mostly based in the southeast and eastern seaboard. SPLC also estimates that about a 191,000 hate crimes happen on US soil per year—of which just 7,000 to 8,000 are reported.

Hate speech is usually considered in context of it being used against people on the basis of their ethnicity, nationality or religion, but it can in theory be used against any group. Puzzlingly and alarmingly, hate speech in the context of gender is often not considered as such or given as much weight as it should be, particularly in light of contexts such as rape, where victims often face disbelief and even blame, either direct or implied ("What was she wearing?" "Was she drunk?"), and abortion stigma, where often already vulnerable women are threatened and harassed, and can be victims of violence. As Katie Gillum of Inroads, an international campaign against abortion stigma, said to me in an interview for another piece on the influence of the US on abortion rights worldwide, "In practice abortion stigma makes seeking or providing abortion a more complicated or dangerous activity, and stigma makes talking about a personal experience more uncomfortable or dangerous."

Susan Benesch, Harvard associate professor and founder of the Dangerous Speech Project, studies how what she refers to as "dangerous speech" can incite mass violence. A former war journalist, she's traveled to faraway places more likely to be found on a Foreign and Commonwealth Office official "essential travel only" list than a holiday brochure, but last October, she expressed concerns about the situation closer to home.

According to the Dangerous Speech Project, which studies dangerous speech and how to prevent violence by counteracting it, "Dangerous Speech" is "uncannily similar" across different languages and cultures. The example they gave is of people often being referred to as insects, vermin, aliens, threats, or pollution. They contend that "Inflammatory public speech rises steadily before outbreaks of mass violence, suggesting that it is a precursor or even a prerequisite for violence, which makes sense: groups of killers do not form spontaneously." There is some historical support for this claim. Jews were called rats and vermin by Nazis before the Holocaust. Tutsi people were called cockroaches by the Hutu before the horrendous 1994 Rwanda genocide.

How, then, does speech become dangerous?

The Dangerous Speech Project believes that countering dangerous speech must not impinge on freedom of speech, and so careful efforts must be made to distinguish it from speech that is merely distasteful. Professor Benesch has developed a framework for identifying when speech stops being merely offensive and becomes dangerous. For that escalation to happen, two of the following five factors must be true:

- A powerful speaker with a high degree of influence over the audience.
- The audience has grievances and fears that the speaker can cultivate.
- A speech act that is clearly understood as a call to violence.
- A social or historical context that is propitious for violence, for any of a variety of reasons, including long-standing competition between groups for resources, lack of efforts to solve grievances or previous episodes of violence.
- A means of dissemination that is influential in itself, for example, because it is the sole or primary source of news for the relevant audience.

Trump, like many politicians, has been difficult to pin down, as many of the things he says are ambiguous. However, Benesch did have concerns that some of his more memorable campaign statements sit a little too comfortably within her framework. It doesn't take a massive stretch of the imagination to read his suggestion that "the Second Amendment people" "do something" about Hillary Clinton, for example, as "a call to violence." "It seems to me impossible that people didn't understand that as a reference to violence," Benesch said to the *Washington Post* in October. Trump's influence over his audience isn't in doubt. His claim in a debate that Obama and Clinton were founders of the Islamic State was, she said in the same interview, a "hallmark of dangerous speech to describe an in-group member as the enemy."

Science backs up the idea that speech can cause deeper wounds at both societal and personal levels than hurt feelings. Neurological and sociological research has proven that hate speech leads to "a dehumanizing effect" which lessens our empathy for other people.

Some neurological theory suggests that pain is an emotional as well as a physical response, and a study in 2004 which used MRI to look at brain responses to stimuli, found that some of the same neurological pathways were activated when a person witnessed another in pain as when that person themselves were in pain. In short, witnessing pain activated the same neural components involved in the emotional experience of pain whether the pain was first-hand or witnessed (the neural components in the physical aspects of pain were unaffected).

Although research in this area, pain empathy, is still relatively new, and more rigorously controlled studies with much larger groups of patients are needed to increase confidence in conclusions drawn from the field, a 2015 review of a number of studies by a lawyer and a neurology professor leads them to hypothesize that: the components of our brains which produce empathy respond best when we witness the pain or suffering of people we consider to be on the same level as us. When we dehumanize people, or see them as a cultural "outgroup," we are less moved by their suffering. An extreme form of this is violence targeted against a specific group, but it also makes us more likely to tolerate and less likely to be disturbed by denial of the rights we ourselves take for granted. The authors of this hypothesis have themselves acknowledged its limitations, such as the shortage of conclusive neuroscience research to rely on. More research on every aspect of hate speech may be urgently required; when I performed JSTOR and Google Scholar searches for studies linking hate speech to actual violence, for example, I was returned few results, many of which were over 20 years old.

On some level, a loyalty to our own group is probably instinctive, and when channeled positively it could even be healthy. If you don't have a lot of money, investing it in your own kids rather than any big ideas, or the whims of a person you don't know very well, is healthy. But when this in group-outgroup effect intensifies to the point that we can hear about violent crimes being afflicted against a fellow human and not be even remotely perturbed, or intensifies further to the point where we can first justify harming others, and then inflict harm without feeling any need for justification to ourselves or society, we no longer live in a safe society.

Equality, and equal safety for all humans, is dependent not only on the law, but also on the empathy everyone in a community has for each other.

It's difficult to think about hate speech, particularly when perpetrated by someone in power, without being reminded of Martin Niemöller's famous "First They Came," in which the narrator describes the groups that the Nazis came for which he did not speak out for, as he was not one of them. The chilling ending is that when they came for the narrator, there was no one left to speak out. That poem has been thought-provokingly re-written for Trump's America.

Hate speech can also cause physical harm to a targeted group caused by the group itself. A study published in the peer-reviewed journal *Psychosomatic Medicine* in 2004 looked at data from the 1950s on 10 ethnic immigrant groups who accounted for approximately 40 percent of all immigration into the United States at that time. The extent to which any of these groups experienced hate speech predicted suicide rates within that group.

In February of 2016, a self-styled "pick-up artist" Roosh V, who insisted that a woman's value was determined by her fertility and beauty and campaigned for the legalization of rape, attempted to arrange a meet-up of like-minded men in a town less than an hour from where I was living at the time. Petitions sprang up in response, with an unsurprising chain of reactions on social media. I quickly noticed that all of my own contacts who responded to calls to ban this man and his meet-ups responded with: "I may not agree with what you say but will defend to the death your right to say it." They were male, white, and for the most part university-educated and economically comfortable. Some of the time, these men were liberal progressives and would be appalled by sexual assault, but they had the luxury of growing up free from the fear of rape, free from any sense that the right to their own bodies might ever be compromised. For them, this man's words were simply disagreeable words—it was an academic consideration. However, I, like many of my female friends, was all too aware that if even one deviant misogynist harboring a latent rape fantasy met someone "like-minded" and felt validated, our streets wouldn't be as safe for us anymore.

However, freedom of speech is a hallmark of a free society, and there's always the difficult question: if we start curtailing speech, where does it stop?

If a relatively liberal government brings in well-intentioned policies to protect vulnerable citizens by curtailing hate speech, what will the next government do with that legislation?

Are freedom of speech and limitation of hate speech fundamentally incompatible?

Not necessarily. Freedom of speech is in many ways an abstract entity, and therefore it's easy to confuse issues. For example, if a white supremacist holds a rally and openly encourages lynching, and that rally is condemned as it should be, what are we criticizing? The extreme racist's right to hold those views and to speak them, or his right to a platform from which he can actively work to incite violence? In an ideal world, everyone has the right to free thought and free speech. But we live in a collective society, and no one has an automatic right to a platform. Society, collectively, should hand megaphones to those who have something positive to contribute, something important to say. And there needs to be some kind of gate-keeping. As a trained scientist, I try keep up with developments through academic journals and well-respected specialist magazines like *New Scientist*, rather than random blogs discovered through late-night google sprees because I trust them to check their facts, and not to publish anything that could cause tangible harm to any group. The risk of causing offense is very, very different to singling out an already vulnerable group and painting massive target signs on their backs.

In an ideal society, anyone can say what they want.

But ideal worlds tend to be much more simplistic than the real thing. Our society is complicated, multi-faceted, has powerful groups and vulnerable groups, groups more and less susceptible to manipulation, and sometimes, in such a complex world, the rights that certain groups view as inalienable come into conflict. A decent society should look to its most vulnerable first, and get its priorities straight. Physical safety must be a higher priority than the right of any bigot to a platform.

Absolute free speech might be a nice idea, but in reality, a society in which a privileged group or person can say things that threaten the safety and fundamental rights of less privileged groups is absolutely not a free society.

The debate around free speech is usually skewed because our most vulnerable and marginalized groups very rarely access the kind of platforms that allow them to broadcast on the same level as the archetypical wealthy white man. In an insightful piece for the *Establishment*, sociologist Katherine Cross notes that "Our First Amendment exists to protect the rights of the ordinary person to criticize those in power without fear of reprisal from the state. Yet instead we debate the right of an already rich man to use his exalted platform to take away the speech rights of others." Ms. Cross further notes that in the proliferation of Voltaire quotes following the cancellation of a Milo Yiannopolis event at the University of California earlier this year, there was considerably "less emphasis on what Yiannopolis was actually at Berkeley to talk about—providing training to young Republicans on how to identify and report 'illegal immigrant students' on the Berkeley campus, a form of harassment which is nothing if not chilling on the speech of those students and potentially damaging to their prospects."

The issue is knowing which speech to curtail, and when someone should be denied a platform. Benesch's framework is potentially valuable, as it lays out when speech stops being merely distasteful and becomes dangerous. It is also more subjective than, for example, a politician censoring his opponents. The Dangerous

Speech Project website states that: "Efforts [to curtail dangerous speech] must not infringe upon freedom of speech, however, since that is a fundamental right and since free speech itself may help to prevent violence. Before acting to limit 'dangerous speech'—speech that catalyzes violence—we must have a means to distinguish it from other speech, even that which is controversial or repugnant."

Some scholars have contended that due to "glorification of freedom of expression" and a lack of effective laws, the US has become something of a haven for hate speech.

It's certainly true that many of us here in Europe were shocked at how blatantly racist and misogynistic many of Trump's campaign statements were. Writing about Canada's hate speech laws, barrister David Butt commented that: "In the United States, even the most hateful, virile and destructive speech is constitutionally protected," whereas in Canada, although hate speech laws do put some limits on freedom of expression, "our constitution protects not only free expression, but multiculturalism and equality as well. So, to read the constitution holistically, we cannot permit one protected freedom to undermine other rights and freedoms enjoying equal status." According to the Southern Poverty Law Centre: "Hate has a First Amendment right. Courts have routinely upheld the constitutional right of the Ku Klux Klan and other hate groups to hold rallies and say what they want."

It may well be time for the US to reconsider its laws as far as the lack of regulation of hate speech is concerned. In the meantime, the Southern Poverty Law center has launched a community response guide detailing how citizens can do their bit to combat hatred, including practical actions, how to get informed, and how to support victims of hate crimes. The guide is based on the SPLC's long experience of working with various groups to combat hate and provides some very encouraging case studies of where their suggestions have worked. As they say:

"Our experience shows that one person, acting from conscience and love, is able to neutralize bigotry. Imagine, then, what an entire community, working together, might do."

Mass Shootings Are Frequently Caused by Extremists

Mehdi Hasan

Mehdi Hasan is a senior columnist at the Intercept *and the host of the podcasts "Deconstructed" by the* Intercept *and "UpFront" by* Al Jazeera English. *He is based in Washington, DC.*

On Saturday morning, a gunman at a Walmart in El Paso, Texas, shot and killed at least 20 people before surrendering to the police. By all accounts, Patrick Crusius, the 21-year-old alleged shooter, is a fan of President Donald Trump and his policies. According to the Southern Poverty Law Center, a "Twitter account bearing the suspect's name contains liked tweets that include a 'BuildTheWall' hashtag, a photo using guns to spell out 'Trump,'" and more.

Incredibly, the nation woke up to more grim news on Sunday, with reports that a man suited up in body armor and bearing a rifle with high-capacity magazines had carried out a rampage in Dayton, Ohio, killing at least nine people and injuring 26.

Little is known yet about the Dayton shooter, but a four-page manifesto authorities believe was written by Crusius and posted shortly before the El Paso attack is full of the kind of hateful rhetoric and ideas that have flourished under Trump.

The manifesto declares the imminent attack "a response to the Hispanic invasion," accuses Democrats of "pandering to the Hispanic voting bloc," rails against "traitors," and condemns "race mixing" and "interracial unions." "Yet another reason to send them back," it says.

Sound familiar? The president of the United States—who condemned the El Paso attack on Twitter—has repeatedly referred to an "invasion" at the southern border; condemned

"After El Paso, We Can No Longer Ignore Trump's Role in Inspiring Mass Shootings," by Mehdi Hasan, First Look Media, August 4, 2019. Reprinted by permission.

Mexican immigrants as "rapists" and Syrian refugees as "snakes"; accused his critics of treason on at least two dozen occasions; and told four elected women of color to "go back" to the "crime infested places from which they came." (It is worth noting that Crusius, in his alleged manifesto, claims his views "predate" and are unrelated to Trump but then goes on to attack "fake news.")

That there could be a link between the attacker and the president should come as no surprise. But it might. Over the past four years, both mainstream media organizations and leading Democrats have failed to draw a clear line between Trump's racist rhetoric and the steadily multiplying acts of domestic terror across the United States. Some of us tried to sound the alarm—but to no avail.

"Cesar Sayoc was not the first Trump supporter who allegedly tried to kill and maim those on the receiving end of Trump's demonizing rhetoric," I wrote last October, in the concluding lines of my column on the arrest of the so-called #MAGAbomber. "And, sadly, he won't be the last."

I wish I could have been proven wrong. Yet since the publication of that piece almost a year ago, which listed the names of more than a dozen Trump supporters accused of horrific violence, from the neo-Nazi murderer of Heather Heyer in Charlottesville to the Quebec City mosque shooter, there have been more and more MAGA-inspired attacks. In January, four men were arrested for a plot to attack a small Muslim community in upstate New York—one of them, according to the Daily Beast, "was an avid Trump supporter online, frequently calling for 'Crooked Hillary' Clinton to be arrested and urging his followers to watch out for Democratic voter fraud schemes when they cast their ballots for Trump in 2016."

In March, a far-right gunman murdered 51 Muslims in two mosques in Christchurch, New Zealand—and left behind a document describing Muslim immigrants as "invaders" and Trump as "a symbol of renewed white identity and common purpose."

And now, this latest massacre in El Paso. Let's be clear: In an age of rising domestic terrorism cases—the majority of which are motivated by "white supremacist violence," according to FBI Director Christopher Wray—Trump is nothing less than a threat to our collective security. More and more commentators now refer, for example, to the phenomenon of "stochastic terrorism"—originally defined by an anonymous blogger back in 2011 as "the use of mass communications to incite random actors to carry out violent or terrorist acts that are *statistically predictable but individually unpredictable.*"

Sounds pretty Trumpian, right? As I wrote in October: "The president may not be pulling the trigger or planting the bomb, but he is enabling much of the hatred behind those acts. He is giving aid and comfort to angry white men by offering them clear targets—and then failing to fully denounce their violence."

And as I pointed out on CNN earlier this year, there is a simple way for Trump to distance himself from all this: Give a speech denouncing white nationalism and the violence it has produced. Declare it a threat to national security. Loudly disown those who act in his name. Tone down the incendiary rhetoric on race, immigration, and Islam.

Trump, however, has done the exact opposite. In March, in the wake of the Christchurch massacre, the president said he did not consider white nationalism to be a rising threat, dismissing it as a "small group of people." A month earlier, in February, Trump was asked whether he would moderate his language after a white nationalist Coast Guard officer was arrested over a plot to assassinate leading journalists and Democrats. "I think my language is very nice," he replied.

In recent weeks, the president has again launched nakedly racist and demagogic attacks on a number of black and brown members of Congress, not to mention the black-majority city of Baltimore. When his cultish supporters responded to his attack on Rep. Ilhan Omar, D-Minn., with chants of "send her back," Trump stood and watched and later referred to them as "patriots."

So we're supposed to be surprised or shocked that white nationalist violence is rising on his watch? That hate crimes against almost every minority group have increased since his election to the White House in 2016?

On Tuesday, just days before this latest act of terror in El Paso, the leaders of the Washington National Cathedral issued a scathing, and startlingly prescient, rebuke of Trump:

> Make no mistake about it, words matter. And, Mr. Trump's words are dangerous.
>
> These words are more than a "dog-whistle." When such violent dehumanizing words come from the President of the United States, they are a clarion call, and give cover, to white supremacists who consider people of color a sub-human "infestation" in America. They serve as a call to action from those people to keep America great by ridding it of such infestation. Violent words lead to violent actions.

Thanks to his hate-filled rhetoric, his relentless incitement of violence, and his refusal to acknowledge the surge in white nationalist terrorism, the president poses a clear and present danger to the people, and especially the minorities, of the United States.

Extremists Use the Internet and Social Media to Radicalize Young People

Federal Bureau of Investigation

The Federal Bureau of Investigation (FBI) is the domestic intelligence and security service of the US government, serving as its principal law enforcement agency.

More and more, violent extremists are trying to radicalize and recruit our nation's youth, especially through the Internet and social media.

It's the FBI's primary responsibility—working with its many partners—to protect the nation from attacks by violent extremists. One important way to do that is to keep young people—the future of our country—from embracing violent extremist ideologies in the first place.

This website is designed to help do just that. Built by the FBI in consultation with community leaders and other partners, it uses a series of interactive materials to educate teens on the destructive nature of violent extremism and to encourage them to think critically about its messages and goals.

The site emphasizes that by blindly accepting radical ideologies, teens are essentially becoming the "puppets" of violent extremists who simply want them to carry out their destructive mission—which often includes targeting or killing innocent people.

The FBI encourages community groups, families, and high schools across the United States to use this site as part of their educational efforts. All Americans are asked to join the FBI in exposing the seductive nature of violent extremist propaganda and offering positive alternatives to violence.

"Don't Be a Puppet: Pull Back the Curtain on Violent Extremism," Federal Bureau of Investigation, https://www.fbi.gov/cve508/dont-be-a-puppet-pull-back-the-curtain-on -violent-extremism-tri-fold-brochure.

Violent extremism is "encouraging, condoning, justifying, or supporting the commission of a violent act to achieve political, ideological, religious, social, or economic goals."

Groupthink

Groups can be a powerful way to bring people together to achieve common goals. Groupthink happens, however, when those in the group stop stating their opinions or using critical thinking because they wish to avoid conflict. This can result in extremely poor decision-making.

Violent extremist organizations are highly vulnerable to groupthink. They are often headed or motivated by a strong leader who is rarely challenged. Different beliefs or ideas are not accepted. Violent extremist groups often work in secret, not only because their activities and plans are illegal, but also because they want to keep out other opinions.

Violent Extremism and Groupthink

Irving L. Janis, a social psychologist who performed important research on groupthink, wrote the words below in a 1972 book. His description of groupthink many years ago sounds very similar to how violent extremists are today:

> The members' firm belief in the inherent morality of their group ... enable them to minimize decision conflicts ... especially when they are inclined to resort to violence. ... "Since our group's objectives are good," the members feel, "any means we decide to use must be good." This shared assumption helps the members avoid feelings of shame or guilt about decisions that may violate their personal code of ethical behavior.

Getting Around Groupthink

Here are a few ways to avoid groupthink:

- Include a mix of people and perspectives in your group.
- Limit the leader's influence at meetings.

- Encourage different opinions.
- Discuss ideas with outside experts.
- Carefully consider all choices before making decisions.

Symbols

A symbol is something that stands for something else. For example, common American symbols—such as the US flag, Statue of Liberty, White House, and bald eagle—represent this country and its freedoms.

A symbol can build pride or create a positive emotional connection. Symbols can also be used to create fear and to control people. Violent extremists have used various symbols over the years to fuel feelings of revenge and hatred. They have also attacked many symbols of America and other countries to make their actions seem more important.

Blame

Extremist groups and individuals often appear in communities struggling with social or political issues. Rather than improving these situations or their own lives through constructive actions, violent extremists often place the blame on another person or group. They argue that the only solution to these problems or injustices is to violently oppose and even destroy those they claim are responsible.

The Blame Game

Placing blame is an effective way to recruit people with feelings of frustration and tum them into a group united by a sense of purpose. It enables extremists to invent an "enemy" that must be destroyed. This makes violence seem like the best solution and even a moral duty.

Distorted Principles

Violent extremists are driven by twisted beliefs and values—or ideologies—that are tied to political, religious, economic, or social goals.

For example:

- Many violent extremist ideologies are based on the hatred of another race, religion, ethnicity, gender, or country/ government.
- Violent extremists often think that their beliefs or ways of life are under attack and that extreme violence is the only solution to their frustrations and problems.
- Despite what they sometimes say, violent extremists often do not believe in fundamental American values like democracy, human rights, tolerance, and inclusion.
- Violent extremists sometimes twist religious teachings and other beliefs to support their own goals.
- Hate crimes are a type of violent extremism. They are directed at a person or group of people because of their race, color, religion, gender, gender identity, sexual orientation, national origin, or disability. These crimes can take many forms— such as burning down a religious building or threatening or injuring another person.
- Hate crimes can be carried out by a single person or by small groups inspired by hateful beliefs. In many cases, an individual may commit a hate crime because of peer pressure. Many violent extremists wrongly blame their hate crimes on their victims, claiming the victims provoked them or were somehow at fault.

What Do Violent Extremists Believe?

Violent extremists have many distorted beliefs that they use to justify violence and hateful attacks. Read a few examples below.

VIOLENT EXTREMIST GROUP	EXAMPLE OF DISTORTED BELIEF
White Supremacy Extremists	Members of inferior races should be killed.
Environmental Extremists	Destroying property and even harming people is needed to protect the environment.
Militia Extremists	The US government is a threat to the people and should be opposed by force.
Religious Extremists	Violent attacks are needed to protect our beliefs from the corrupting influence of certain people or countries.
Anarchist Extremists	Society needs no government or laws. Violence is necessary to create such a society.

Propaganda

Violent extremists often use propaganda—misleading or biased information that supports a particular point of view—to trick people into believing their ideologies. It's the primary extremist recruiting tool, and you could be a target. The goal of propaganda is to create a compelling story that people will buy into by twisting the facts.

Channels and Messages

Extremist propaganda can be found anywhere, but violent extremists today often use online tools like e-mail, social media, websites, forums, and blogs. You could also hear violent extremist propaganda directly from a friend, relative, or community or religious leader.

- Western Nations Are Corrupt and Must Be Destroyed
- Our People Are Being Oppressed. No One Is Doing Anything. We Must Fight Back.

- Our Race and Traditions Are Superior. To Save Our People from Ruin, We Must Eliminate All Those Who Disagree.
- You Can't Trust Government or Law Enforcement. Arm Yourself and Be Ready to Fight.
- The Environment Is Under Attack. We Must Stop This Abuse Through Economic Sabotage and Guerrilla Warfare.

What Are Known Violent Extremist Groups?

Groups that commit acts of violent extremism can have very different beliefs and goals. They are located in many countries around the world. Most have websites or use social media, so they can now reach and recruit people just about anywhere.

Keep in mind that some of those who carry out extremist attacks and hate crimes are only loosely motivated by these groups and may not be actual members.

Please note: You may know someone in this country who has radical beliefs or agrees with the actions or ideologies of violent extremist groups. That is their right under the US Constitution. However, if a person seriously plans to carry out an act of violence or is strongly pushing you or someone else to do so, that is illegal.

International Violent Extremist Groups

More than 50 violent extremist groups around the world have been named terrorist organizations by the US government. Just six of the many groups identified by the US State Department are listed on the left. Thousands of violent extremists belong to these groups, support their beliefs, or are inspired by them.

Al Qaeda

Overview of Group: Al Qaeda, which means "The Base" in Arabic, is a global extremist network started in 1988 by the now deceased Osama bin Laden. It seeks to free Muslim countries from the influence of Western countries and attacks Muslim nations that don't agree with its version of the Islamic religion.

Who or What They Target: Al Qaeda attacks those it believes are enemies of Islam. In 1988, al Qaeda said that it is the duty of its followers to kill Americans and citizens of other countries that support the United States. Al Qaeda has carried out many bombings and other acts of violence, including the attacks of September 11, 2001.

Al Shabaab

Overview of Group: Al Shabaab is a violent extremist organization based in Somalia that seeks to replace the current government through violence. Al Shabaab has recruited dozens of US citizens to train and fight with them.

Who or What They Target: Al Shabaab has carried out many bombings and murders in Somalia and in nearby countries like Kenya. It not only targets government officials and military troops but also Somali peace activists, international aid workers, police officers, and others. Al Shabaab has a history of kidnapping and hurting women and girls.

Hizballah

Overview of Group: Hizballah, or "Party of God," is an extremist group based in Lebanon. Hizballah supports the global rise of Shia, a branch of Islam, and it is inspired by the Iranian revolution. Hizballah also supports certain Palestinian groups in their struggle against Israel.

Who or What They Target: Hizballah targets Israel and its supporters, including the United States. Hizballah and its partners are responsible for some o f the deadliest extremist attacks against the US in history, including the bombing of a Marine base in Lebanon in 1983 that killed more than 250 Americans. Hizballah has supporters worldwide, including in the United States.

ISIL/ISIS

Overview of Group: ISIL (DAESH) is a highly violent extremist group that has killed thousands of men, women, and children, mostly Muslims. The group calls itself the "Islamic State," but its members follow an extreme, fringe interpretation of Islamic law.

They do not represent mainstream Islam, and the vast majority of Muslims are horrified by their actions. ISIL members work to enslave or kill anyone who disagrees with them and have taken over parts of Iraq and Syria. ISIL continues to actively recruit US citizens, especially young people.

Who or What They Target: ISIL has attacked the people of Iraq, Syria, and other nations—including government and military officials as well as journalists and school children. ISIL also has targeted Americans and has killed US troops and civilian hostages.

Kahane Chai

Overview of Group: Kahane Chai ("Kahane Lives") was started by the son of a radical Israeli-American rabbi named Meir Kahane, who was killed in 1990. The group seeks to expand the borders of Israel.

Who or What They Target: Kahane Chai has targeted Arabs, Palestinians, and Israeli government officials. Its last major attack was in 1994, when a Kahane Chai supporter opened fire at a mosque in the southern West Bank, killing 29 people.

Revolutionary Armed Forces of Colombia (FARC)

Overview of Group: Fuerzas Armadas Revolucionarias de Colombia ("Revolutionary Armed Forces of Colombia"), or FARC, is a violent rebel group. Since it was created in 1964, FARC has tried to overthrow the Republic of Colombia, South America's oldest democracy. It also sends a lot of illegal drugs into the US and other countries.

Who or What They Target: FARC mostly targets the people and government of Colombia through bombings, murder, and other attacks. FARC sees US citizens as "military targets" and has kidnapped and murdered several Americans in Colombia.

Domestic Extremist Ideologies
Violent extremists based in the United States have different beliefs that lead them to commit crimes and acts of violence. Some of the most common domestic ideologies are listed here. It is important

to note that it is legal to have hateful or extremist beliefs as long as you don't commit crimes or violence based on those beliefs. The right to assemble (or gather) in groups is also protected by the US Constitution.

Sovereign Citizen Extremists

What They Believe: Sovereign citizens believe they are separate or "sovereign" from the United States even though they live here. They think they don't have to answer to any government authority. Sovereign citizens use their beliefs to justify fraud and other non-violent crimes. But some sovereign citizen extremists turn to violence and commit murder, threaten public officials, and destroy property as part of their anti-government, anti-tax beliefs.

Who or What They Target: Sovereign citizen violent extremists usually target members of the government—including judges, police officers, and tax officials. In 2010, for example, a sovereign citizen extremist killed two Arkansas police officers during a routine traffic stop.

Abortion Extremists

What They Believe: Some abortion extremists believe that violence and bloodshed are justified to support their different beliefs on abortion. These violent extremists have turned to murder, bombings, assault, vandalism, kidnapping, and arson. They have also made death threats and sent hate mail and suspicious packages.

Who or What They Target: Violent anti-abortion extremists have targeted women's reproductive clinics and the health care professionals and staff who work in these facilities, including doctors, nurses, receptionists, and even security guards. In one case in 2009, for example, a Kansas doctor who performed abortion services was shot and killed in his local church by an anti-abortion extremist. Those who use violence to defend abortion rights have murdered, threatened, and attacked those who oppose abortion.

Animal Rights Extremists and Environmental Extremists

What They Believe: Some animal rights and environmental extremists believe violence is needed to stop those they think are hurting animals or the environment. These violent extremists usually don't seek to kill or injure people, but their crimes—which include property damage, vandalism, threats, cyber attacks, arson, and bombings—have caused millions of dollars in damages and disrupted the lives of many Americans.

Who or What They Target: Violent animal rights extremists attack those they believe are linked to the abuse of animals. Typical targets include the fur industry, companies and individuals involved in animal research, and businesses that ship animals. Violent environmental extremists target those they believe are destroying the environment, such as businesses and individuals involved in construction or automobile sales.

Militia Extremists

What They Believe: A militia is a group of citizens who come together to protect the country, usually during an emergency. Some militia extremists, however, seek to violently attack or overthrow the US government. Often calling themselves "patriots," they believe the government has become corrupt, has overstepped its constitutional limits, or has not been able to protect the country against global dangers.

Who or What They Target: Violent militia extremists mainly target those they believe could violate their constitutional rights, such as police officers and judges. In one 2010 case, a Michigan militia group planned to kill a police officer and later attack the parade of cars in the funeral, hoping to start a large battle. The FBI and its partners stopped them from carrying out their plan.

White Supremacy Extremists

What They Believe: White supremacy extremists are motivated by a hatred of other races and religions. Some try to achieve their political and social goals through violence. These violent extremists often wrongly believe that the US government is hurting the country or secretly planning to destroy it.

Who or What They Target: White supremacy violent extremists target the federal government and racial, ethnic, and religious minorities. Their methods have included murder, threats, and bombings. As just one example, white supremacists attacked a pair of Middle Eastern men on New Year's Eve in 2011, punching one victim in the face and head.

Anarchist Extremists

What They Believe: Anarchist extremists believe that society should have no government, laws, or police, and they are loosely organized, with no central leadership. Violent anarchist extremists believe that such a society can only be created through force.

Who or What They Target: Violent anarchist extremists usually target symbols of capitalism they believe to be the cause of all problems in society—such as large corporations, government organizations, and police agencies. They damage property, cause riots, and set off firebombs. In some cases, they have injured police officers.

Why Do People Become Violent Extremists?

No single reason explains why people become violent extremists, but it often happens when someone is trying to fill a deep personal need. For example, a person may feel alone or lack meaning and purpose in life. Those who are emotionally upset after a stressful event also may be vulnerable to recruitment. Some people also become violent extremists because they disagree with government policy, hate certain types of people, don't feel valued or appreciated by society, or think they have limited chances to succeed.

Personal Needs

Just about everyone wants to be happy and feel like they make a difference in life. Meeting these needs through violent activities is not the answer. See how unmet needs could lead to radicalization.

PERSONAL NEED	DESCRIPTION	RISK IF NEED NOT MET
Power	Feeling in control of life may lead to improved self-confidence or a sense of importance.	Those who wish to control or feel superior to others may be attracted to violent extremism.
Achievement	Mastering skills and accomplishing goals can provide a feeling of self-worth.	Those who want to make a positive difference in life may falsely think that they can do that by taking part in violent or hateful attacks.
Affiliation	Having close relationships helps create a feeling of well-being and belonging.	Those who are looking for new friends may wrongly believe that they can find beneficial companionship in violent extremist groups.
Importance	Feeling significant and worthy of respect helps develop a person's self-image.	Those who seek recognition and attention may turn to violent extremism, even if it means hurting other people.
Purpose	Believing in a higher calling or mission can give meaning and direction in life.	Those looking for purpose in life may be drawn to the clear-cut yet twisted ideologies of violent extremism.
Morality	Having a strong set of beliefs can guide a person's decisions, especially in difficult times.	Those who are afraid of different viewpoints and lifestyles may be attracted to violent extremism or hate groups.
Excitement	Having a new adventure can make life seem more interesting and inspiring.	Violent extremism may offer a false promise of excitement and glamour to those who are bored with life.

Fears and Frustrations

Violent extremists may also try to recruit you by tapping into your personal problems. Remember that everyone experiences difficult emotions. Seek help or be supportive of others going through a tough time.

Social Alienation

Those who feel isolated can sometimes be easily convinced by violent extremist beliefs. Don't become a puppet for violent extremists by joining groups that want to hurt others just so you feel less alone. Consider healthy ways you can connect with others, including people that share your interests.

Anxiety

Teens can be stressed by problems at home, grades, peer pressure, bullying, and other issues. Blaming other people, groups, or the government is not a good way to cope with your anxiety, so don't become a puppet for violent extremist groups that do this. Look for other ways to reduce stress, such as talking to friends or exercising.

Frustration

It is natural to feel frustrated or angry when you are treated unfairly or rejected by others. But don't become a puppet for violent extremists to create an outlet for your anger and revenge. Find peaceful, constructive ways of dealing with feelings of frustration.

Painful Experiences

Painful experiences—including physical or emotional abuse, a romantic breakup, or the loss of a loved one—can upset a person and lead to lifelong challenges. Don't become a puppet for violent extremist groups just to mask your pain or grief. Seek help from a parent, teacher, or professional.

Extremists Already Have Bigoted and Hateful Beliefs—Online Hate Speech Is Just an Expression of Them

Megan Ross, Brooks Hepp, and Kianna Gardner

The three authors are former fellows of the Center for Public Integrity. Megan Ross was an Ethics and Excellence Journalism Fellow. Brooks Hepp was a Myrta J. Pulliam Fellow. Kianna Gardner was a Don Bolles Fellow.

Ken Parker was baptized in a predominantly black church in Jacksonville, Florida, his tattoos—a large swastika, one Confederate flag, a Ku Klux Klan insignia and an Iron Cross—immersed in holy water.

Less than five months earlier, Parker had been a regional director of the National Socialist Movement, and before that, a grand dragon of the Ku Klux Klan. His duties included littering neighborhoods with recruitment fliers and screaming "White power!" into a megaphone at rallies.

In April, Parker resigned from the NSM and issued a statement that read, in part, "I am convinced that what I have been committed to for the last several years is hurting my walk with God … I can't keep on living this life."

"Love thy neighbor as thyself," said Parker, quoting the bible during an interview with News21. "It doesn't differentiate between the Jewish neighbor, a Mexican neighbor, a black neighbor. It says love thy neighbor as thyself."

But Parker is an anomaly.

According to the Southern Poverty Law Center, an advocacy group that tracks hate and bigotry toward marginalized communities, there were at least 950 active hate groups in the

United States in 2017, up from 917 the previous year. Experts say the term "hate group" is increasingly difficult to define, as extremist groups grow in number, diversify in ideology and use codewords to spread their messages.

Parker said he became involved in far-right groups because he said he was missing a sense of identity and camaraderie.

"I did 11 years in the Navy on submarines, and I definitely felt the brotherhood," Parker said. "So you get out of there and you're unemployed, and you're lucky if you qualify for unemployment for two months. And it's like, 'Aw, I'm kind of missing this sense of belonging, so I can join the Klan and get some rank and some belonging.'"

Arno Michaelis, a former racist who's now an anti-extremism activist, was a member of the Northern Hammerskins in the late 1980s and early '90s. The group is a chapter of Hammerskin Nation, whose website states, "We must secure the existence of our people and a future for White Children."

Michaelis said recruiters for extremist groups target white people—often working class and ex-military—who believe they've been victimized and short-changed by society.

"So that's what we would do," he said, "is look for ways that people were suffering, look for whatever is wrong in their life, and then we would try to spin that problem into our narrative and invite them in as a means to addressing that problem."

Scott Shepherd is a former grand dragon of the KKK who joined at a young age, though he had been cared for during his childhood by a black woman who is now 103. Born into a family with a dysfunctional alcoholic father, he said he joined the Klan as a teenager.

"A lot of them [leaders of the Klan] put their arm around me and said 'We're taking care of you. We know you had a hard life.' I fell for it. Hook line and sinker. And that's how I got started with the Klan."

About 25 years ago, he decided to quit: "Racism is like an addiction or habit. They are hard to break and you still slip up occasionally. But finally, the habit gets broken."

For decades, the groups that make up the far-right have capitalized on fear, offering a sense of belonging to those who feel disenfranchised, Michaelis said.

"So it's like, 'Well, even in this horrible world where everything is out to get you and all these bad things are happening, like your race is something that will always connect you,'" Michaelis said. "Your race is something that will always be there for you, and by the way, your race is completely threatened by everyone else on Earth.'"

According to the Census Bureau's 2017 National Population Projections, non-Hispanic white people will make up just less than half the population of the United States by 2045.

"We are fastly becoming a minority in the country we founded," said Jason Kessler, an organizer of the 2017 Unite the Right rally in Charlottesville, Virginia, which was called to protest plans to remove a statue of Gen. Robert E. Lee, hero of the Confederacy.

This fear of becoming a minority is one commonly shared among far-right extremists, regardless of otherwise differing ideologies.

"I think they're scared they're going to lose everything they've worked for, their standing in society and everything that's dear to them," said A.J. Marsden, assistant professor of psychology at Beacon College in Leesburg, Florida. "In our culture, it has been traditionally easier for white people to get good jobs, for them to go to school, to get a good education, et cetera, and I think they start to see their opportunities narrow."

Michaelis said the reinforcement of this fear is key to the radicalization process.

"All white-power ideology stems from the idea that white people are oppressed," he said. "And therefore anything goes in order to fight this oppression, the same way that anyone else who felt oppressed would justify fighting against what they see as their oppressors."

The term "far-right" broadly describes those whose political beliefs lie at the most conservative end of the political spectrum, including groups that exist to protect "white interests," said Mark Pitcavage, a senior research fellow with the Anti-Defamation League's Center on Extremism. The far-right also includes anti-government groups and single-issue groups, such as anti-Muslim extremists.

The Southern Poverty Law Center's Extremist Files outline defining characteristics of ideological groups within the far-right. White supremacists believe in the biological superiority of the white race and feel white people should hold a privileged position in a multi-ethnic society.

White nationalists favor the creation of a white ethnostate, or a homeland for white people, instead of a multi-ethnic society. Many extremists, including Richard Spencer of the National Policy Institute and Jeff Schoep of the National Socialist Movement, have said they support a nonviolent ethnic cleansing, in which minorities would be compensated for moving from the proposed homeland. Others endorse more forceful tactics.

In 2008, Spencer coined the term "alternative-right" or "alt-right" to describe one of the newer ideological groups in the far-right. Alt-right members believe their white identity is threatened by multicultural influences and frequently ridicule "political correctness."

"Some of the more extreme groups out there don't really get along with the alt-right because they feel like the alt-right is too soft, too willing to engage with mainstream conservatives. It's too compromised," said Benjamin Lee, senior research associate at the Centre for Research and Evidence on Security Threats, an advocacy group that tracks hate and bigotry toward marginalized communities.

Lee said the alt-right's internet trolling makes it difficult to tell whether alt-right members are serious or not, a characteristic that contrasts them with more traditional extremist groups who trace their roots back to the early 20th century.

The Ku Klux Klan began as a vigilante group of former Confederate soldiers aiming to intimidate former slaves and other blacks after the Civil War. The group identifies itself today as a Christian "civil rights for whites" organization.

Neo-Nazi groups assume the prejudices and symbolism of Adolf Hitler's National Socialist German Workers Party, which ruled Germany from 1933 to 1945. Like the Nazis, the neo-Nazis share a deep hatred of Jews and intolerance of gays, lesbians and transgender people and non-whites.

Many far-right extremist groups have adapted their public images in recent years to appeal to more mainstream, modern audiences, according to group leaders. Among them is the National Socialist Movement, which is headquartered in Detroit. The NSM is one of the largest and most prominent neo-Nazi groups in the country, according to the Southern Poverty Law Center.

The group's commander, Jeff Schoep, said he dislikes the term "neo-Nazi" to describe the beliefs of the group, adding that members are reducing their invocation of Nazi-German symbols.

In November 2016, Schoep said the group was undergoing a "cosmetic overhaul," but he assured members, "your Party Platform remains the same, your Party remains unchanged."

"The same movement you saw in the 1970s that was putting out some of those cartoons and racially insensitive materials or things like that would have appealed to a demographic in the '70s," Schoep said. "Now, it's not something we use. I want to change with the times."

In 2008, the group retired its "Brownshirt" uniforms, which closely resembled Nazi paramilitary uniforms worn before World War II, and instituted all-black "battle dress uniforms," according to Schoep.

In November 2016, the NSM ceased public use of the swastika, which had previously been the centerpiece of their flags, banners and uniforms. It was replaced by the Othala Rune, another symbol used by German Nazis but one that's far less provocative in modern America.

"We are attempting to separate the bad labels from the second World War and try to make this a little more American," said Harry Hughes, public relations director for the NSM. "So we're attempting to make this a little more American-looking and less German-looking."

The group's web domain, however, still includes the number "88," a shorthand substitute for the phrase "Heil Hitler" (H being the eighth letter of the alphabet).

Many other extremist groups lost their domains when website-hosting companies cracked down after last summer's Unite the Right rally in Charlottesville. Schoep said the NSM can't be kicked off its internet platform because the group hosts its own website.

But those who are removed from major hosting platforms, like GoDaddy, can turn to alternative platforms that usually don't censor websites.

Neo-Nazi Gerhard Lauck, has spent years providing such a platform through his website-hosting company Zensurfrei, German for "censorship free." Zensurfrei hosts hundreds of sites from the US and parts of Europe, Lauck said.

"Gerhard has created a small corner of that world that is very hospitable to various actors and speakers," said Bob Wolfson, former regional director of the Anti-Defamation League in Omaha, Nebraska.

Although many extremist groups focus on increasing their online reach, Billy Roper, a self-described white nationalist and founder of the ShieldWall Network, a community of race-war "preppers," emphasizes the need for more visible demonstrations of free speech.

"Unfortunately, the internet sometimes discourages actual activism because people are too content to just sit, click and clack on the keyboard all day without actually being in person, but we're trying to change that a little bit," he said.

Roper encourages physical meetings of members of the far-right, from private gatherings to public rallies. Rallies, however, can become violent when far-right extremist groups are confronted by counterprotesters.

But Lee, with the Centre for Research and Evidence on Security Threats, said the leaders of most extremist groups are not violent themselves, rather, it is the fringe members—such as James Alex Fields, who's charged with murder in the death of a counterprotester at the Unite the Right rally in Charlottesville. Authorities say Fields, who traveled to Virginia from Ohio, rammed his car into a crowd, killing Heather Heyer, 32, and injuring dozens.

"We each tend to carry around a very general definition of the far-right," Lee said. "Most of them are actually nonviolent, but we tend to focus on the outliers."

Schoep said the NSM brings riot shields to their events, not because they want to be violent, but because they need to protect themselves from groups known as "antifa," far-left counterprotesters who often engage in violence at far-right rallies.

"All of us were covered in urine because the antifa likes to throw urine balloons, feces balloons," Schoep said. "There were chemicals. I had something that was burning my skin."

Michaelis, the reformed skinhead, takes issue with antifa tactics and said such violent opposition only reinforces the fears that fuel far-right groups.

"When people violently oppose them, i.e., antifa, that is the single most powerful way to keep their members galvanized and part of the group and violent and attacking other people," Michaelis said.

He said it was the people who treated him with undeserved kindness that ultimately motivated him to reject racism.

"Nobody ever beat the Nazi out of me," Michaelis said. "It wasn't violence and hate that led me from the movement. It was people who were very brave, who were able to respond to my hatred with kindness and with compassion."

Hate Speech Is in the Eye of the Beholder

Kim R. Holmes

Kim R. Holmes is executive vice president at the Heritage Foundation. He previously served on the State Department's Defense Policy Board. He holds a PhD in history from Georgetown University.

Intolerance and illiberalism, nakedly defined as abstractions or principles, are seldom if ever outwardly embraced by progressives. None but the most extreme will argue that intolerance and censorship are good things in themselves. Normally the preferred course is more subtle.

Instead of openly arresting people who say the wrong things, the new purveyors of intolerance try to sublimate their prohibitions on speech, expression, and thought into more popularly accepted channels. Something must be done to make these prohibitions more palatable, because there is still a great deal of respect in America for freedom of thought, speech, and expression.

How to do that? The answer is quite simple: Change the subject. Shift the gaze away from the sanctity of speech to something more wholesome—to the feelings of minorities, for example, or to the supposed desire to live in more diverse communities.

One of the most popular strategies is to carve out a special category of speech that, in theory at least, leaves the rest of free speech alone. If this can be done, speech can be regulated and criminalized without involving a direct assault on the First Amendment.

A prime example of parsing good speech from bad is the notorious notion of "hate speech," which involves designating certain kinds of remarks, gestures, expressions, and writings as intentionally hateful and thus worthy of regulation and even criminalization.

"The Origins of 'Hate Speech,'" by Kim R. Holmes, The Heritage Foundation, October 22, 2018. Reprinted by permission.

Attempts to prohibit hate speech and hate crimes have been around for years in the United States. Appropriate efforts to condemn symbolic acts of violence such as cross burnings by the Ku Klux Klan have expanded over the years to include all sorts of alleged speech and thought crimes.

Today a public statement against illegal immigration or same-sex marriage can be labeled hate speech. The Southern Poverty Law Center routinely includes pro-family groups in its list of "hate" groups based solely on their opposition to same-sex marriage.

By and large America's upper courts have not looked favorably on campaigns to criminalize speech. When such cases have come before the Supreme Court, it has ruled in favor of free speech.

Nevertheless, proponents of hate speech restrictions are not giving up. The movement has grown in recent years, particularly as the values and ideologies of identity politics became acceptable to more Americans.

Legal Restrictions on Speech

There are two types of threatening or defamatory speech that can potentially be restricted by the law. One is any speech, gesture, or conduct that is intended to incite, and is likely to incite, imminent lawless action such as violence.

The second includes certain classes of speech, such as obscenity and libelous words, which can be limited. They were not considered to rise to the level of First Amendment protected speech.

Oliver Wendell Holmes added a twist to the theme of prohibited speech in 1919 when he argued in *Schenck v. United States* that "falsely shouting fire in a crowded theater" was prohibited. The circumstances for restricting speech were expanded somewhat, but the main purpose of preventing physical harm was retained.

Every attempt to curb free speech in America has run up against the First Amendment, which provides clearly that "Congress shall make no law … abridging the freedom of speech, or of the press … ."

Yet the First Amendment is not the only obstacle. There is also the tendency in American jurisprudence to observe what is called the "strict scrutiny" test of the law. The least restrictive means available should be used to pursue a certain end. In addition, laws should be narrowly tailored to deal with conduct that pertains to a relevant end.

When it comes to connecting intentions and actions, the law should focus on what can clearly be discerned. It must also be very careful not to allow extraneous factors to cloud judgment about whether a crime was committed.

The Rise of "Hate Speech" Rules

Criminal intent has always mattered in determining if a crime was premeditated. All this started to change with the rise of radical multiculturalism. Under its influence the ideas of hate speech and hate crimes were invented. Instead of worrying about the violent intent of individuals, hate speech advocates wanted to ban utterances, gestures, conduct, or writing that they deemed prejudicial against a protected individual or group.

They were most successful on college campuses, spawning a rash of new speech codes and other imaginative methods to control what people say and think. In the name of diversity certain classes of people—racial minorities, women, and homosexuals—were considered to need protection from offensive language.

The shift was not to some heightened awareness of persecution so much as a new focus on generalizing the causes of the persecution. Hate speech no longer focused on the acts of individuals but on whole classes of people who were supposedly to blame, regardless of what individuals in each class might say or believe.

Despite their success on campus, advocates for hate speech restrictions have been rebuffed repeatedly by the courts. One well-known case is the high court's 1977 decision ruling that the City of Skokie, Illinois, violated the First Amendment when it passed a series of ordinances designed to prevent demonstrations by American Nazis without affording strict procedural safeguards.

Another case involved a St. Paul, Minnesota, teenager's burning of a makeshift cross on an African-American neighbor's lawn in 1990. He was convicted of violating St. Paul's Bias-Motivated Crime

Ordinance, but his conviction was overturned in a 1992 unanimous decision by the Supreme Court on free speech grounds.

As the courts closed the doors on hate speech laws, advocates sought other windows of opportunity.

The most successful has been to try to control speech through administrative regulation, such as enlisting the Federal Communications Commission to regulate the content of speech on radio, TV, and other broadcast media.

The first attempt was the so-called Fairness Doctrine of 1949, whereby political content on the airways would supposedly be balanced by regulation. The Fairness Doctrine has been overturned, but in 1992 Congress directed the National Telecommunications and Information Administration to examine the role of telecommunications in disseminating hate speech as an incitement to hatred and violence. In 1993 the National Telecommunications and Information Administration issued a report titled "The Role of Telecommunications in Hate Crime," in which it argued that a "climate" of hate can be seen as an inducement to violence.

These attempts to regulate free speech directly have been no more successful than attempts to curtail speech through the courts. But that does not mean the hate speech movement has been a failure. Its most significant impact has been on public and political opinion—on expanding the acceptable boundaries for defining what free speech actually is.

By the time of the Oklahoma City bombing in 1995, the ground had already been prepared to bring hate speech norms and concepts into popular political discourse. It was then that President Bill Clinton tried to place blame for the Oklahoma attack on the "loud and angry voices of hate," by which he was widely interpreted to mean conservatives and Republicans.

Under this new standard, people who had nothing to do with a crime could be held accountable for it, at least indirectly and politically. It was a subtle but important step toward blurring the lines between actions and speech, and between individual culpability and the social "climate" in which crimes are thought to take place.

Since the 1990s, under the influence of the radical multicultural movement, the definitions of hate speech have become far more elastic. In 2009, the National Hispanic Media Coalition outlined its definition in a report. It specified four areas as hate speech: false facts, flawed argumentation, divisive language, and dehumanizing metaphors.

Hate speech was no longer about the explicit words of individuals meant to incite violence, but a general atmosphere of public opinion that could be construed to encourage violence against certain kinds of people.

Seeing Speech as Harm

There are very serious problems with the concept of hate speech. For one thing, it fails to distinguish between legitimate political content, which is protected by the Constitution, and explicit intentions to commit violence, which are not.

Under the new rules, what may clearly be an expression of political opinion could be interpreted as offensive to anyone anywhere, and therefore arbitrarily deemed hateful. No direct threats of harm are even necessary. Certain ideas and opinions are now defined by their political content to be the moral equivalent of a threat to do violence and physical harm.

The motive of hatred is inferred not from actual words threatening violence but from, for example, what the National Hispanic Media Coalition deems "false facts, flawed argumentation, and divisive language." No distinction is made between threatening someone with real violence and merely disagreeing with the facts and arguments. Nor is allowance made for the possibility that a disagreement over facts and logic may have nothing whatsoever to do with feelings of hatred.

Hating someone and criticizing their arguments or positions are not the same thing. A Christian, for example, may object to gay marriage on religious grounds, but that does not mean he hates any individual gay person any more than a gay person's objection to the traditional definition of marriage means he hates straight people.

To assume that all disagreements are grounded in irrational fears is itself irrational. If it were otherwise, we might as well abolish not only our universities but our system of law: Both rely on the assumption that people are moral beings with the freedom to make choices. Without that assumption, people honestly could not be held accountable for anything.

If it were all about presumed ill motives, especially those mandated by vague social forces, we might as well not bother to learn the facts about anything. Our pursuit of knowledge and justice fundamentally depends on open and honest debate, and to sacrifice that standard is not only to return to pre-liberal standards of controlling knowledge but to slide over into authoritarian methods of thought control.

Losing Objectivity

Another serious flaw is that hate speech laws completely ignore a fundamental principle of American jurisprudence—namely, that a person convicted of a crime must have actual criminal intent.

It is ludicrous to argue that saying offensive words alone or simply disagreeing with someone in an argument shows criminal intent. Even in cases where maliciousness was clearly involved, such as the St. Paul case, the Supreme Court has ruled that freedom of speech trumps offensive speech when no physical harm is intended.

It also has ruled that criminal intent is required even in cases where violent language is aimed at a specific person. It is not enough, the high court ruled in the 2015 Facebook case of Anthony Elonis, to show that a "reasonable" person could detect a threat from someone's postings. The mental state of the person making a threat must be considered to determine whether the real intent to commit violence existed.

Proponents of hate speech restrictions such as New York University Professor Jeremy Waldron believe that criminal intent to commit violence is irrelevant. All that is required for speech to be categorized as hate speech is that a person's or group's "dignity" is under threat.

Put aside the huge difference between offending someone and meaning them physical harm. The bigger problem is that it is left almost entirely to the accuser to determine and apply the standards for defining dignity and therefore establish what is offensive and what is not.

The rational give-and-take that one assumes should be part of such determinations—and which necessarily presumes some social consensus on how the speech affects the public good—is short-circuited by giving one side a decided advantage.

The problem is compounded by the fact that there can be legitimate disagreements over the political content of speech. Nor can the determination of hate speech be justified solely on the basis of whether doing so engenders "social peace," as Waldron argues.

If this were an unassailable public good in and of itself, we could find any number of authoritarian ways to try to enforce it. But we would be considerably less free and democratic as a result.

Authoritarian rulers ban free speech to maintain public order, but even if this extreme case is not what Waldron and other defenders of hate speech have in mind, we must ask where to draw the line.

Should the people at the Council on American-Islamic Relations get to decide that any criticism of Sharia law is ipso facto "Islamophobia" and therefore make it legally prohibited?

Where is the threat to public order here? Surely it is not from people who object to the religious coercion demanded by Sharia law, but rather from those who use coercion (1) to maintain religious discipline among the faithful and (2) to muzzle those outside the faith who may have religious views of their own.

If peace is about justice, there is precious little justice in that.

Not since George Orwell's "thoughtcrimes"—the author's word for unapproved thoughts in his novel *1984*—has there been so little regard for the dangers of controlling free speech.

Not only has the bar been lowered from threatening physical violence to merely giving offense, it is now up to those who allege an offense to decide whether the offense was intended.

The presumption of guilt is built ideologically into the structure of the political narrative underlying the accusations: Only racial minorities can know what it is like to be discriminated against, so only they can know what hate speech is. Only Muslims get to decide what "Islamophobia" is and what it is not.

What is really in the heart of the accused is immaterial, because both meaning and intent are prejudged by a set of proscribed ideological positions and, in some cases, even by the race of the accused.

The Death of Freedom

Whatever this may be, it is not liberal. Liberalism of all kinds, including the more progressive variety adopted by the ACLU in the 20th century, always made freedom of expression and speech a constitutionally protected principle.

Not anymore. Today free speech is in progressive liberal circles clearly subordinated to other concerns. Lost are not only a sense of balance and proportion but the principle of mediation.

Liberalism has survived all these years because it was flexible. It accepted implicitly the idea that people had different interests as individuals, and that the only way to reconcile those differences was to assume the good faith of everyone equally as individuals.

Hate speech theory does not do that. It assumes bad faith on the part of people regardless of their stated intentions, essentially calling them liars if they defend themselves against the current orthodoxy.

Above all, hate speech theory obliterates the ethical responsibility of the individual. Liberal philosopher and lawyer Ronald Dworkin was quite right that, as obnoxious as some hateful speech can be, it is necessary to allow it for no other reason than that trying to ban it will undermine the moral case against discrimination.

Ultimately people—individual people—have to make their own moral judgments about how to treat each other with respect and dignity. Having this issue forced on them by law and coercion not only takes away the right of individuals to make that call on their own, it also undermines the moral authority of making the right decision.

As John Locke argued in his *Letter Concerning Toleration* (1689), coercion in matters of conscience can undercut the moral legitimacy of the oppressor's cause. One must be free to decide; otherwise the decision is not ethical at all but simply a matter of submission as a way to avoid punishment.

Am I exaggerating the threat to free speech? Most Americans still cherish free speech. They will not give it up lightly. But the trends are not good.

Look at what is happening in other countries. Most European countries and Canada have had very strict hate speech laws for quite some time. Most of them are far more intrusive in criminalizing the content of speech and expression than we are used to in the United States.

For example, in Sweden a pastor arrested in 2003 was sentenced to one month in prison for delivering a sermon in church critical of homosexuality. The conviction was eventually overturned on free speech grounds, but what opened the door for the prosecution in the first place was a 2002 law that explicitly listed criticism of sexual orientation in church sermons as a criminal act.

The abuse happened because the law was written with little or no regard for religious liberty, which may not be surprising in a highly secular country like Sweden, but which should be a scandal in the United States.

One of the unique attributes of being American has been a passionate devotion to free speech. It is one characteristic that sets us apart from other Western countries, where the tradition is far less cherished.

As lines get blurred and free speech is cheapened as a mere social fiction by clever intellectuals, we could find ourselves losing one of the most precious birthrights of our historical fight for freedom—the liberty to believe and say what we please about the nature of our government, our politics, and our society.

Taking Down Websites Does Not Stop Hate Groups—It Just Gives Them More Attention

Thomas Holt, Joshua D. Freilich, and Steven Chermak

Thomas Holt is an associate professor of criminal justice at Michigan State University, where Steven Chermak is a professor of criminal justice. Joshua D. Freilich is a professor of criminal justice at the John Jay College of the City University of New York.

In the wake of an explosion in London on September 15, President Trump called for cutting off extremists' access to the internet.

Racists and terrorists, and many other extremists, have used the internet for decades and adapted as technology evolved, shifting from text-only discussion forums to elaborate and interactive websites, custom-built secure messaging systems and even entire social media platforms.

Our research has examined various online communities populated by radical and extremist groups. And two of us were on the team that created the US Extremist Crime Database, an open-source database helping scholars better understand the criminal behaviors of jihadi, far-right and far-left extremists. Analysis of that data demonstrates that having an online presence appears to help hate groups stay active over time. (One of the oldest far-right group forums, Stormfront, has been online in some form since the early 1990s.)

But recent efforts to deny these groups online platforms will not kick hate groups, nor hate speech, off the web. In fact, some scholars theorize that attempts to shut down hate speech online may cause a backlash, worsening the problem and making hate

"Can Taking Down Websites Really Stop Terrorists and Hate Groups?" by Thomas Holt, Joshua D. Freilich, and Steven Chermak, The Conversation, September 15, 2017, https://theconversation.com/can-taking-down-websites-really-stop-terrorists-and-hate-groups-84023. Licensed under CC BY-ND 4.0.

groups more attractive to marginalized and stigmatized people, groups and movements.

Fighting an Impossible Battle

Like regular individuals and corporations, extremist groups use social media and the internet. But there have been few concerted efforts to eliminate their presence from online spaces. For years, Cloudflare, a company that provides technical services and protection against online attacks, has been a key provider for far-right groups and jihadists, withstanding harsh criticism.

The company refused to act until a few days after the violence in Charlottesville. As outrage built around the events and groups involved, pressure mounted on companies providing internet services to the Daily Stormer, a major hate site whose members helped organize the demonstrations that turned fatal. As other service providers stopped working with the site, Cloudflare CEO Matthew Prince emailed his staff that he "woke up … in a bad mood and decided to kick them off the internet."

It may seem like a good first step to limit hate groups' online activity—thereby keeping potential supporters from learning about them and deciding to participate. And a company's decision may demonstrate to other customers its willingness to take hard stances against hate speech.

But that decision can cause problems: Prince criticized his own role, saying, "No one should have that power" to decide who should and shouldn't be able to be online. And he made clear that the move was not a signal of a new company policy.

Further, as a sheer practical matter, the distributed global nature of the internet means no group can be kept offline entirely. All manner of extremist groups have online operations—and despite efforts by mainstream sites like Facebook and Twitter, they are still able to recruit people to far-right groups and the jihadist movement. Even the Daily Stormer itself has managed to remain online after being booted from the mainstream internet, finding new life as a site on the dark web.

Drawing Attention

Efforts to knock extremists offline may also have counterproductive results, helping the targeted groups recruit and radicalize new members. The fact that their websites have been taken down can become a badge of honor for those who are blocked or removed. For instance, Twitter users affiliated with IS who were blocked or banned at one point are often able to reactivate their accounts and use their experience as a demonstration of their commitment.

When a particular site is under fire, people who hold similar beliefs may be drawn to support the group, finding themselves motivated by a perceived opportunity to express views that are opposed by socially powerful companies or organization. In fact, radicalization scholars have found that some extremist groups actively seek out harsh penalties from criminal justice agencies and governments, in an effort to exploit perceived overreactions for a public relations advantage that also aids their recruitment efforts.

Relations Between Tech Companies and Police

Internet companies' decisions about online expression also affect the difficult relationship between the technology industry and law enforcement. There are, for example, many examples of cooperation between web hosting providers and police investigating child pornography or other crimes. But policies and practices vary widely and can depend on the circumstances of the crime or the nature of the police request.

For example, Apple refused to help the FBI retrieve information from an iPhone used by a man who shot 14 people in San Bernardino, California, in 2015. The company said it wanted to avoid setting a precedent that could put its customers at risk of intrusive or unfair investigations in the future. And Apple has since substantially increased its protections for data stored on its devices.

All of this suggests the tech industry, law enforcement and policymakers must develop a more measured and coordinated approach to the removal of extremist and terrorist content online. Tech companies may intend to be creating a safer and more inclusive environment for users—but they may actually encourage radicalization and simultaneously create precedents for removing content in the face of public outcry, regardless of legal or moral obligations.

To date, these concerns have arisen suddenly and briefly only in the wake of specific events, like 9/11 or Charlottesville. And while opponents may shut down one or more hate sites, the site will likely pop back up elsewhere, maybe even stronger. The only way to really eliminate this kind of online content is to decrease the number of people who support it.

CHAPTER 4

Should Hate Groups and Hate Speech Be Illegal?

Overview: Hate Speech Is Not Clearly Demarcated from Free Speech

Stephen J. Wermiel

Stephen J. Wermiel is a professor of practice of constitutional law at American University Washington College of Law. He is the past chair of the Civil Rights and Social Justice section of the American Bar Association.

Freedom of speech, Supreme Court Justice Benjamin Cardozo declared more than 80 years ago, "is the matrix, the indispensable condition of nearly every other form of freedom." Countless other justices, commentators, philosophers, and more have waxed eloquent for decades over the critically important role that freedom of speech plays in promoting and maintaining democracy.

Yet 227 years after the first 10 amendments to the US Constitution were ratified in 1791 as the Bill of Rights, debate continues about the meaning of freedom of speech and its First Amendment companion, freedom of the press.

This issue of *Human Rights* explores contemporary issues, controversies, and court rulings about freedom of speech and press. This is not meant to be a comprehensive survey of First Amendment developments, but rather a smorgasbord of interesting issues.

One point of regular debate is whether there is a free speech breaking point, a line at which the hateful or harmful or controversial nature of speech should cause it to lose constitutional protection under the First Amendment. As longtime law professor, free speech advocate, author, and former American Civil Liberties Union national president Nadine Strossen notes in her article, there has long been a dichotomy in public opinion about free speech. Surveys traditionally show that the American people have strong

"The Ongoing Challenge to Define Free Speech," by Stephen J. Wermiel, American Bar Association. Reprinted by permission.

support for free speech in general, but that number decreases when the poll focuses on particular forms of controversial speech.

The controversy over what many call "hate speech" is not new, but it is renewed as our nation experiences the Black Lives Matter movement and the Me Too movement. These movements have raised consciousness and promoted national dialogue about racism, sexual harassment, and more. With the raised awareness come increased calls for laws punishing speech that is racially harmful or that is offensive based on gender or gender identity.

At present, contrary to widely held misimpressions, there is not a category of speech known as "hate speech" that may uniformly be prohibited or punished. Hateful speech that threatens or incites lawlessness or that contributes to motive for a criminal act may, in some instances, be punished as part of a hate crime, but not simply as offensive speech. Offensive speech that creates a hostile work environment or that disrupts school classrooms may be prohibited.

But apart from those exceptions, the Supreme Court has held strongly to the view that our nation believes in the public exchange of ideas and open debate, that the response to offensive speech is to speak in response. The dichotomy—society generally favoring free speech, but individuals objecting to the protection of particular messages—and the debate over it seem likely to continue unabated.

A related contemporary free speech issue is raised in debates on college campuses about whether schools should prohibit speeches by speakers whose messages are offensive to student groups on similar grounds of race and gender hostility. On balance, there is certainly vastly more free exchange of ideas that takes place on campuses today than the relatively small number of controversies or speakers who were banned or shut down by protests. But those controversies have garnered prominent national attention, and some examples are reflected in this issue of *Human Rights.*

The campus controversies may be an example of freedom of speech in flux. Whether they are a new phenomenon or more numerous than in the past may be beside the point. Some part of the current generation of students, population size unknown, believes that they should not have to listen to offensive speech that targets oppressed elements of society for scorn and derision. This segment of the student population does not buy into the open dialogue paradigm for free speech when the speakers are targeting minority groups. Whether they feel that the closed settings of college campuses require special handling, or whether they believe more broadly that hateful speech has no place in society, remains a question for future consideration.

Few controversies are louder or more visible today than attention to the role and credibility of the news media. A steady barrage of tweets by President Donald Trump about "fake news" and the "fake news media" has put the role and credibility of the media front and center in the public eye. Media critics, fueled by Trump or otherwise, would like to dislodge societal norms that the traditional news media strives to be fair and objective. The norm has been based on the belief that the media serves two important roles: first, that the media provides the essential facts that inform public debate; and, second, that the media serves as a watchdog to hold government accountable.

The present threat is not so much that government officials in the United States will control or even suppress the news media. The Supreme Court has probably built enough safeguards under the First Amendment to generally protect the ability of the news media to operate free of government interference. The concern is that constant attacks on the veracity of the press may hurt credibility and cause hostility toward reporters trying to do their jobs. The concern is also that if ridicule of the news media becomes acceptable in this country, it helps to legitimize cutbacks on freedom of the press in other parts of the world as well. Jane E. Kirtley, professor and director of the Silha Center for the Study of Media Ethics and Law at the University of Minnesota and past director for 14 years of the Reporters Committee for Freedom of the Press, brings her expertise to these issues in her article.

Other current issues in our society raise interesting free speech questions as well. It is well-established law that the First

Amendment's free speech guarantee only applies to government action. It is the government— whether federal, state, or local—that may not restrict freedom of speech without satisfying a variety of standards and tests that have been established by the Supreme Court over the past century. But the difference between government action and private regulation is sometimes a fine line. This thin distinction raises new questions about freedom of speech.

Consider the "Take a Knee" protests among National Football League (NFL) players expressing support for the Black Lives Matter movement by kneeling during the National Anthem. On their face, these protests involve entirely private conduct; the players are contractual employees of the private owners of the NFL teams, and the First Amendment has no part to play. But what could be more public than these protests, watched by millions of people, taking place in stadiums that were often built with taxpayer support, debated by elected politicians and other public officials, discussed by television commentators because of the public importance of the issue. That is not enough to trigger the application of the First Amendment, but should it be? First Amendment scholar David L. Hudson Jr., a law professor in Nashville, considers this and related questions about the public-private distinction in his article.

Another newly emerging aspect of the public-private line is the use of social media communications by public officials. Facebook and Twitter are private corporations, not government actors, much like NFL team owners. But as one article exams in this issue, a federal court recently wrestled with the novel question of whether a public official's speech is covered by the First Amendment when communicating official business on a private social media platform. In a challenge by individuals who were barred from President Trump's Twitter account, a federal judge ruled that blocking access to individuals based on their viewpoint violated the First Amendment. If the ruling is upheld on appeal, it may open up an entire new avenue of First Amendment inquiry.

One aspect of current First Amendment law is not so much in flux as in a state of befuddlement. Courts have long wrestled with how to deal with sexually explicit material under the First Amendment, what images, acts, and words are protected speech and what crosses the line into illegal obscenity. But today that struggle that has spanned decades seems largely relegated to history because of technology. The advent of the relatively unregulated Internet has made access to sexually explicit material virtually instantaneous in the home without resort to mailed books and magazines or trips to adult bookstores or theaters.

In his article, law professor and First Amendment scholar Geoffrey R. Stone elaborates on much of the legal and social history and current challenges in handling sexually explicit material, drawing on his own 2017 book, *Sex and the Constitution: Sex, Religion, and Law from America's Origins to the Twenty-First Century*.

If there is a unifying theme in the articles in this issue of *Human Rights*, it may be that while as a nation, we love our freedoms, including freedom of speech and freedom of the press, we are never far removed—even after more than two centuries—from debates and disputes over the scope and meaning of those rights.

The Rise of Incels Shows the Danger of Tolerating Hate Groups

Tony Nagy

Tony Nagy is a former journalist and political adviser.

It's a bit of a shock when normally sober voices such as those of academic Carol Johnson and the *Sydney Morning Herald* political editor Peter Hartcher start using the term "authoritarian" about Australia.

We see our nation as balanced and fair, with an anti-authoritarian ethos—thanks to war story legacies and legendary diggers famed for an Aussie spirit driven by laconic humour and a healthy cynicism around power and those who wield it.

So are we really losing this? And if we mindlessly follow the paths of those increasingly vocal "strongmen" leaders currently ruling other nations, from Orban's Hungary to Trump's America and Britain's Boris, are we likely to suffer a similar fate of becoming a "softer" version of an authoritarian state here in Australia?

The testiness of recent public debates, particularly around climate change and bushfires, has highlighted how easy it is to deploy the language of division. And whilst Prime Minister Scott Morrison has recently sought to lower the intensity of the fractious debate, he has not been without clear and strategic skill in stoking anger. His speeches on laws to stop legal protest, and even lawful investing, would be remarkable in any other political times. Such would be the heavy handedness of a command state.

Not to mention his constant refrain: "Whose side are you on?," which naturally posits two opposing camps.

This is in stark contrast to his political hero, John Howard, who—for all his capacity for wedge politics—was firm in his often stated belief that there is "more that unites us than divides."

Well, apparently no more.

Anger Is a Bit Like Climate Change

It's become a bit of a lazy trope to say that the rise of feminism had led to an emasculation of men's traditional roles and rendered males somehow weakened and vulnerable.

Nevertheless, there are an increasing number of young men who not only believe this, but who self-identify with this kind of "victimhood."

The tragic irony of course is the opposite. Rigid masculinity is a health hazard, and as we experience a state of flux it's easier to attack the apparent problem—feminism and women seeking equality—rather than the deep structural constant of patriarchy, which is the ultimate determinator of power in society, not just of power between the sexes but also power within male hierarchies.

Dr. David Duriesmith argues that masculinity and its structures pose the greatest threat to men and their mental and physical health:

"Changing gender norms have been traumatic for many men and resulted in a profound sense of loss among many," he says. "The structural conditions around work, marriage and politics are all shifting in ways that weaken men's dominance."

"Work in the United States has suggested that these shifts have left many young men feeling like they exist in a state of limbo. Due to increased casualisation and a breakdown of manufacturing in the Global North, young men often feel that they cannot transition into a stereotypical form of adult manhood."

We need to pay heed to those words. As Australia's economy has dramatically reformed over the last four decades, these forces apply here, and with even more force since the Global Financial Crisis.

In this light, it's possible to see men as victims—rather than perpetrators—of patriarchy. For much like the feudal strata—and postmodern capitalism seems ever more returning to its feudal roots in all but name, given the enormous disparities in wealth where 26 people control 50% of the world's wealth—at no stage is a unemployed or underemployed male on the same level as one of the Koch brothers: despite some similarities in anatomy.

In that sense anger is a bit like the long run impacts of climate change: the environment gets gradually more and more prone to extreme results, although at the time it may appear there's little to be seen.

Breeding Cohorts of Anger: The Rise of the Incels and the Alt-Right

The internet has created a space for autodidacts, but also spaces for cult-like self-indoctrination. Is there really much difference between a terrorist training to join ISIS or a white supremacist group in Australia wanting to set up white enclaves, to so-called incels who join chat rooms to share endless grievances about their lack of potency?

In rudimentary terms they are all screaming out their powerlessness in ever more angry language.

But deeds first arise out of ideas and sharing increasingly extreme language.

It may be perverse, but the term "incel" first was coined by a Canadian woman in the 90s, a portmanteau to reflect "involuntarily celibate."

The term first appeared on obscure chat rooms for the shy or socially awkward. Sometime in the early 2000s it metastasised to become a rallying call for males who felt rejected by women and blamed women for their isolation. A Reddit forum later became a particularly active incel community, a place where men blamed women for their "involuntary celibacy," advocating misogyny, violence and rape.

What followed were a spate of shootings and murders, most infamously the mass killings by Elliot Rodgers, who shot six people dead, wounded 14 others and then killed himself. Rodgers identified as an incel. For some he is known as a "saint" and there are even memes with his face superimposed on images of Christ.

Today, incels are being cultivated by white supremacists and members of the alt-right, as foot soldiers to their cause.

From terminology such as "black pills" (referring to women as irredeemably cruel, shallow and egocentric), through to incels who have twisted the Pareto principle to justify their view that 80% of women go out with the top 20% of men, we are talking about a psychology of mass delusion, self-hate and fear.

Before getting too lost down this rabbit hole, some sobering words from the *New York Times*: involuntary celibacy is an adaptation of the idea of male supremacy. The Southern Poverty Law Center (SPLC) describes the subculture as "part of the online male supremacist ecosystem," which they began including in their list of hate groups in 2018. The *New York Times* wrote that "the group has evolved into a male supremacist movement made up of people—some celibate, some not—who believe that women should be treated as sexual objects with few rights."

No wonder *The Handmaid's Tale* seems more documentary than drama.

That said, however, incels are more likely to be victims of patriarchy than feminism. The question is, how do we engage with this group so they are not abandoned to more sinister forces?

Or is that as naive as believing we need civil society?

Conclusion

Powerlessness and fear are a dangerous mix.

Politicians are adept in the language of power, fear and grievance, and some are masterful at using such language to corral votes and public support. Authoritarian figures by definition use hierarchy to create a perception of security—on their terms.

As the commentator Cas Mudde observes in his new book *The Far Right Today*, no country is immune to far right politics, with its form shapeshifting easily between populism, authoritarianism and nativism. Australia has no guaranteed immunity from these forces.

Ultimately men don't need patriarchy to gain any genuine sense of potency. This is why it is more urgent than ever to kick start public discussion about healthy masculinity, while also unpacking its corollary—toxic masculinity.

The very existence of our civil society and democracy may well depend on it.

Laws Should Stop Hate Groups Before They Commit Violent Acts

Jamie Grierson

Jamie Grierson is the home affairs correspondent for the Guardian. *He was shortlisted for the British Journalism Awards. He is based in London.*

A new law allowing for hate groups to be designated and punished before they turn to violence is needed in order to tackle far-right extremists, according to a report by Tony Blair's thinktank, which also seeks powers to ban marches and media appearances.

Generation Identity, a racist movement that promotes a conspiracy theory that white people are being replaced by non-whites in Europe, would be among the groups targeted by new legislation, the Tony Blair Institute for Global Change report said.

The law could sit alongside proscription powers, banning groups concerned with terrorism, but would not be directly linked to violence or terrorism. Rather, it would designate hate groups as organisations that spread intolerance and antipathy towards people of a different race, religion, gender or nationality, the report said.

Offences related to designation as a hate group should be treated as civil, not criminal, the thinktank recommends.

The authors acknowledge that the issue of linking violent and nonviolent extremism is contentious and steps would need to be taken to protect free speech. The recommendations and conclusions are based on analysis of the overlap between four "nonviolent" far-right groups—Britain First, For Britain, the British National Party (BNP) and Generation Identity England—and the ideology of the terrorist Anders Breivik, who murdered 77 people in Norway in 2011.

"New Law Needed to Take On Far-Right Extremism, Says Blair Thinktank," by Jamie Grierson, Guardian News & Media Limited, August 27, 2019. Reprinted by permission.

Writing in a foreword, the former home secretary Jacqui Smith, the chair of the Jo Cox Foundation, said: "The growth of far-right extremist groups and the threat they pose cannot be left on the 'too difficult' pile.

"While ad hoc action has been taken against some groups and the intelligence services are now prioritising the monitoring of far-right terrorists, we need to return to the vexed problem of how to identify the link between violent and nonviolent extremism, and develop a coherent policy approach to tackling the threat of far-right groups."

The government, public agencies and security services have taken steps to tackle far-right violence, but action against nonviolent activity has been limited and uncoordinated.

In its report, "Narratives of Hate: The Spectrum of Far-Right Worldviews in the UK," the thinktank found that public messages from the four activist groups in the UK had shared themes with the world view of Breivik. Victimisation, fundamental conflict between the west and Islam, anti-establishment sentiment and the justification of violence were all found in social media statements by the four UK groups and in statements by Breivik.

Generation Identity and the BNP shared identical world views with Breivik on the theme of victimisation, including ideas of "white genocide" and "the great replacement" theory.

The security services and the government have recognised the threat of violent and non-violent far-right extremism in the UK. MI5 took over the matter from police in 2018, meaning the far right was officially designated as a major national security threat.

In 2016, the neo-Nazi group National Action became the first far-right group to be proscribed in the UK. Announcing the decision, the then home secretary, Amber Rudd, said the group was a "racist, antisemitic and homophobic organisation which stirs up hatred, glorifies violence and promotes a vile ideology."

The ban, which covers three National Action splinter groups, has resulted in several former members being put on trial. To date, National Action is the only far-right group outlawed in the UK.

The Tony Blair Institute has called for a working definition of extremism, which could be used as a tool by government, law enforcement and institutions to tackle individuals and groups that spread hateful ideas but fall short of advocating violence.

It is also calling for further efforts to curb far-right hate online, including working with social media companies to define the limits of acceptable content.

Azmina Siddique, a policy adviser at the institute, said: "These groups are far from innocuous. Only last month, Generation Identity England activists gathered outside the Tower of London dressed as Isis militants and simulated the beheading of two anti-racism activists. It is time that policymakers acted—by defining extremism and designating hateful groups—to stop such obviously malicious acts."

Lady Williams, the minister for countering extremism, said: "Far-right extremism has absolutely no place in our society. Our counter-terrorism and counter-extremism strategies tackle the scourge of both violent and nonviolent far-right extremism head on.

"We have also established the independent commission for countering extremism, which provides advice in what is needed to tackle extremism and will be refreshing our counter-extremism strategy to ensure we keep pace with the evolving threat."

Free Speech Does Not Guarantee Extremists the Right to a Platform

Nesrine Malik

Nesrine Malik is a columnist for the Guardian *and a panelist on the BBC's* Dateline London. *She was born in Sudan and is based in London.*

The Home Office doesn't often get it right—but by declining to indulge the muddled preciousness that surrounds the freedom of speech debate, it has done so. In the space of a fortnight, four extreme-right figures have been turned away at the UK border. The latest was the founder of the German far-right group Pegida. On Monday Lutz Bachmann was denied entry to the UK, and deported. He had been due to give a speech at Speakers' Corner in London's Hyde Park in London, but his presence was deemed "not conducive to the public good."

Bachmann was to have addressed a "free speech" rally. It's not clear how this was different to any other rally, other than by framing any opposition to it as censorship. Characters such as Bachmann are no innocents practising their freedom of speech: they are cynical exploiters of it. They're little better than loiterers waiting round the corner to jump on your windshield, pretending to be hurt, shaking you down for money. It's a scam, trading notoriety and worse for attention. Why do we fall for it?

Most freedom of speech debates now start on the false premise that denying someone a platform is censorship. So we must begin with the correct one, which is that freedom of speech is freedom from punishment. If you are not being convicted and penalised by the state for speaking, then you have freedom of speech. If just one channel of speech has been denied to you, you still have freedom of speech. We're not talking pulping *Lady Chatterley's Lover* here. The

"Hate Speech Leads to Violence. Why Would Liberals Defend It?" by Nesrine Malik, Guardian News & Media Limited, March 22, 2018. Reprinted by permission.

disappeared of Egypt, the jailed and flogged blasphemers of Saudi Arabia, the arbitrarily detained bloggers and journalists of China are being denied freedom of speech. It's an insult to their ordeals that we equate them with shutting down Milo Yiannopoulos's Twitter account. Over the past month, while travelling in north Africa, I was unable to access a host of mainstream news sites that had been blocked by national governments. That is censorship. This is not that complicated.

But it's the "thin end of the wedge," we're told. If we start banning those whose views we don't like, what next? In general, one should be suspicious of "what next?" arguments, because they assume that humans are incapable of behaving in calibrated ways that don't inevitably lead to some future state of fascism. We could extend the right to platform and rally to all, but what next? Paedophile rallies? That's obviously absurd, but it highlights the fact that there are limits, and they are broadly dictated by how much certain values are coded within society. The reason free speech proponents are not out there fighting to hear from child abusers or some radical Muslim clerics is because society or the law regulate the more unpalatable or illegal views away before we have to deal with them at Speakers' Corner.

In *On Liberty*, John Stuart Mill, one of the great defenders of free speech, says a struggle always occurs between the competing demands of authority and liberty. He argues that we cannot have the latter without the former: "All that makes existence valuable to anyone depends on the enforcement of restraints upon the actions of other people. Some rules of conduct, therefore, must be imposed—by law in the first place, and by opinion on many things which are not fit subjects for the operation of law."

But we're far from that. Freedom of speech is no longer a value. It has become a loophole exploited with impunity by trolls, racists and ethnic cleansing advocates. They are aided by the group I call useful liberals—the "defend to the death your right to say it" folk. The writer Mari Uyehara calls them the "free speech grifters," those "who flog PC culture as a singularly eminent threat to the freedom of expression." To them, the "what next?" argument foresees apocalyptic harm that might befall liberal values. It cares much less about speech we can link to violence, or that which compromises the safety of others.

Last Sunday Tommy Robinson, the former leader of the English Defence League, whose social media posts were cited repeatedly in the trial of the Finsbury Park terrorist Darren Osborne, gave the speech at Speakers' Corner that would have been delivered by one of those denied entry—the Austrian Martin Sellner, a leader of the white supremacist group Generation Identity. Useful liberals have swallowed two freedom of speech myths whole: the redefinition of the term to encompass not only freedom from persecution but the right to a platform; and the delusion that freedom of speech is a neutral principle uncontaminated by history or social bias. There are hard choices here. Too often, those who should know better argue for the wrong ones. They fight to their deaths to defend the rights of Bachmann, Sellner and the other peddlers of hate—but not mine.

Better Enforcement of Anti-Hate Laws Would Be More Effective Than More Laws

Stuart Thomson

Stuart Thomson is a politics reporter for the National Post. *He is based in Ottawa, Canada.*

P eople inclined to express hatred online need to be educated about the consequences of their words, members of parliament heard Thursday.

Information campaigns should go both ways, informing people how to report a hateful incident, but also educating potential perpetrators about the laws they may be breaking, said New Democratic Party MP Tracey Ramsey.

"I don't think a lot of people who are expressing this online are aware that what they're doing could be criminal behaviour," Ramsey said.

She told the House of Commons justice committee that she sees a lot of public information campaigns—on bus shelters and in newspapers, for example—about issues like marijuana legalization, but not for education on how to report hate crime. Representatives from a variety of groups agreed that public awareness was vital to make sure people report these incidents.

The testimony was part of an effort by MPs to study online hate after a recent jump in incidents noted by Statistics Canada. The 47 per cent increase in police-reported hate crimes between 2016 and 2017 was largely a result of a spike in non-violent hate crimes in Canada.

Mukhbir Singh, the president of the World Sikh Organization of Canada, said there is real concern in the Sikh community, especially in the wake of an arrest in British Columbia after comments were

"People Need to Be Told That Expressing Hate Online Is Illegal, Justice Committee Hears," by Stuart Thomson, *National Post*, May 2, 2019. Material republished with the express permission of National Post, a division of Postmedia Network Inc.

made about a "pressure-cooker bomb" at Surrey's Vaisakhi parade last week.

"Unfortunately, instances of violence and hatred are not new for the Sikh community," Singh said.

Liberal MP Nathaniel Erskine-Smith, a vice-chair on the privacy and ethics committee, which has also studied the issue, said in an interview that anti-defamation and hate-speech laws are difficult to police online, which encourages some people to behave as if there are no laws.

"In a perfect world, people would be accountable for their own actions and words," said Erskine-Smith, but social media platforms that allow this kind of behaviour, and profit from it in the process, need to be held accountable too.

"The real conversation, what we're really looking at, is just enforcing existing laws," said Erskine-Smith.

All of the panellists at the justice committee hearing said that reports would go up if people were better informed about how to make them.

Emmanuel Duodu, the president of the Ghanaian Canadian Association of Ontario, said the only way hate crime legislation can be effective is if people are empowered and informed.

"Sometimes there is legislation there, but people don't understand it. They don't know their rights," Duodu said.

"Laws around online hate need to be communicated to the community in language that is acceptable and inclusive," said Queenie Choo, the head of SUCCESS, a post-arrival service for immigrants in British Columbia. "If they don't understand the process they will be reluctant to intervene or make a report."

The panellists acknowledged the internet has enabled hate groups to congregate online and even plan violent acts.

"They've been buoyed or bolstered by the idea that there are other people in the world that feel the same way," said Daniel Cho, the moderator for the Presbyterian Church in Canada. These online connections introduce a "wave of legitimacy, and that's a very key problem," he said.

"There are very few people who acknowledge that their actions or speech are motivated by hate. They would not acknowledge themselves to be a hateful person," said Cho. "I'm tempted to quote Dr. Phil that you can't change what you don't acknowledge."

Ramsey said it was "extremely disturbing" that white nationalists are reported to be organizing violent acts on Discord, a chat app for gamers, for example.

Liberal MP Colin Fraser said the problem was complicated by state actors looking to sow disharmony and division in Canada with online hate speech.

David Matas, the senior legal counsel for B'nai Brith Canada, said that's something Jewish people experience around the world, especially with regards to Holocaust denial. It could require a global effort to combat it, he said.

"When you're dealing with international phenomena you need international assistance," Matas said.

B'nai Brith revealed last week that it had recorded 2,041 incidents of anti-semitism in Canada in 2018, which is a 16.5 per cent increase over the previous year. Eighty per cent of those incidents took place on online platforms, like Facebook and Twitter.

Free Discourse Is Necessary for Society to Function, Even If Some Perspectives Are Disagreeable

William Anderson

William Anderson is a tutor, freelance writer, and science teacher.

Imagine a life where you had no freedom to speak what was on your mind, and imagine what it would be like to live in a world like this. Noam Chomsky, a linguistics professor at the Massachusetts Institute of Technology is a big supporter with the idea of free speech. He is known across the globe for his activism and outspoken criticism. He is also said to be "the most often cited living author" and "one of the most respected and influential intellectuals in the world." Chomsky is very respected in the area of free speech, which is why so many people criticize him as well, because he does have some extreme forms of free speech which he thinks how it should be. To show the view Chomsky has, there is one very extreme example of what he thinks should be allowed in society today.

In the year 1979, a French professor of literature named Robert Faurisson published two letters in *Le Monde.* These letters had statements about how gas chambers used by the Nazis in World War 2 to get rid of people of the Jewish faith did not exist. After publishing these letters, there was a huge outrage almost worldwide. Faurisson was convicted for Defamation and also fined and given a prison sentence. A man by the name of Serge Thion, a French Libertarian socialist and Holocaust denier asked Noam Chomsky to sign a petition along with hundreds of other people who signed it to support Faurisson's right to freedom of speech. After Chomsky had signed the petition, people were already attacking him. Jewish-French historian Pierre Vidal-Naquet saw this petition to be a legitimization of Faurisson's denial of the Holocaust and also as a misrepresentation of his intentions. Because Chomsky signed the petition, he also wrote an essay called "Some Elementary Comments on the Rights of Freedom of Expression," which was very critical of the French intellectual response. This also stated that Chomsky did not support Faurisson's ideas but strictly his right to freedom to speech. This essay however was used by Faurisson in his book, which intended to defend his rather obscure views. Vidal-Naquet attacked Chomsky in his essay and thinks Chomsky could have signed other petitions defending the right to freedom of speech without presenting Faurisson as a legitimate historian. Chomsky has stated that he believes in the absolute freedom of speech and also states, "I see no anti-Semitic implications in the denial of the existence of gas chambers or even the denial of the Holocaust."

The example of Faurisson is a clear picture to show Chomsky's view on free speech. Chomsky explains what freedom of speech should be by saying "it is a truism, hardly deserving discussion, that the defense of the right of free expression is not restricted to ideas one approves of, and that it is precisely in the case of ideas found most offensive that these rights must be most vigorously defended." Noam Chomsky strongly believes that everyone has the right to freedom of speech, even that of people who we do not agree with. Chomsky, being Jewish himself, supported Faurisson and his right to that freedom, which people interpreted as him supporting his ideas, which is false. Chomsky signs petitions all the time trying to support the peoples freedom of speech.

A question that can be raised from all this is, can Chomsky's understanding of free speech be allowed in today's society? The answer is yes it can be allowed, and should be allowed. Every day people are discriminated by other people because of what they think and what their opinions are on different topics. If someone doesn't agree with something you say or think, that shouldn't mean you should not have the right to express yourself. Although sometimes it could be dangerous depending on the topic you're arguing or talking about, because there are some people in society today that think there is only one side to things. Faurisson was a Holocaust denier, and even though many people disagreed with him and his ideas, they supported his right to speak what was on his mind and get his opinions across. The fact that he was considered anti-Semitic and given a fine and sentence in prison is ridiculous. He is not hurting anyone when he is doing his own research and trying to look for alternative sources and opinions. By not knowing all opinions and narrowing your knowledge on all topics, you can't really make a reasonable decision on what you think is right without knowing both sides. After 9/11 there were many opinions expressed that didn't agree with each other, and the ones that the Americans didn't like were somehow in some shape or form put aside, ignored, or penalized for having a different thought than the majority of the population. It might take some adjusting and such to get used to the absolute freedom of speech, but without it we're shielding ourselves from other ideas that could prove to be good and interesting as well. If two people were to get into a fight at a school, and no witnessess were around to see it, the principle would listen to both sides most likely before making a decision on what he or she believes. This can be related to the idea of free speech, and Chomsky's understanding of it, in which if you don't hear both sides of things, how can you make an honest decision on what's right and wrong, or what should be or shouldn't be.

The world would be a much different place if people weren't allowed to express their thoughts and were only given stuff to think about, instead of actually looking into things and understanding the whole situation. Without freedom of speech many great philosophers and other great beings would not have made a difference in the world. Martin Luther King Jr. expressed his thoughts and made a difference to millions of people for the better, even when at the time many of thousands of people did not agree with him and were actually mad at him. Same thing with Bob Marley, he spoke his mind on how everyone should get along and be able to express themselves, even after getting shot at he still stood by what he believed. There are so many examples where individuals around the world made a difference by speaking up and questioning things even when people frowned upon it. Without this freedom, society would be very dull and probably not as harmonized as it could be. Chomsky's understanding might be extreme, but with a little effort, it could be allowed in our society today and good would come from it.

Attempts to Limit Extremism Can Restrict Religious Expression

Anthony H. Cordesman

Anthony H. Cordesman is the Arleigh A. Burke Chair in Strategy at the Center for Strategic and International Studies (CSIS), a US-based global think tank.

It is far too easy to focus on individual acts of terrorism and extremism, and ignore the global patterns in such violence. The Burke Chair at CSIS has assembled a wide range of indicators that help quantify and explain these patterns, and that look beyond the crises of the moment to examine longer term trends. They include a range of tables, graphs, and maps that help put the global patterns of terrorism in perspective, and that show the relationships between extremist and terrorist movements, the reject of such movements by the vast majority of Muslims, and the critical role that Muslim states play as strategic partners in the fight against such movements.

Putting the Links Between Islam and Violent Extremism in Context

Any analysis of the patterns in terrorism faces major challenges simply because of the lack of reliable and comparable data, and the tendency to compartmentalize analysis to deal with given threats, nations, and regions. The problem becomes much greater when the analysis attempts to deal with issues as controversial as the links between Islam, extremism, and terrorism.

It is far too easy for analysts who are not Muslim to focus on the small part of the extremist threat that Muslim extremists pose to non-Muslims in the West and/or demonize one of the world's great religions, and to drift into some form of Islamophobia—blaming

"Islam and the Patterns in Terrorism and Violent Extremism," by Anthony Cordesman, Center for Strategic and International Studies, October 17, 2017. Reprinted by permission.

a faith for patterns of violence that are driven by a tiny fraction of the world's Muslims and by many other factors like population, failed governance, and weak economic development.

It is equally easy to avoid analyzing the links between extremist violence and Islam in order to be politically correct or to avoid provoking Muslims and the governments of largely Muslim states. The end result is to ignore the reality that most extremist and terrorist violence does occur in largely Muslim states, although it overwhelmingly consists of attacks by Muslim extremists on fellow Muslims, and not some clash between civilizations.

If one examines a wide range of sources, however, a number of key patterns emerge that make five things very clear:

- First, the overwhelming majority of extremist and violent terrorist incidents do occur in largely Muslim states.
- Second, most of these incidents are perpetrated by a small minority of Muslims seeking power primarily in their own areas of operation and whose primary victims are fellow Muslims.
- Third, almost all of the governments of the countries involved are actively fighting extremism and terrorism, and most are allies of Western states that work closely with the security, military, and counterterrorism forces of non-Muslim states to fight extremism and terrorism.
- Fourth, the vast majority of Muslims oppose violent extremism and terrorism.
- Fifth, religion is only one of many factors that lead to instability and violence in largely Muslim states. It is a critical ideological force in shaping the current patterns of extremism, but it does not represent the core values of Islam and many other far more material factors help lead to the rise of extremism.

The analysis draws on a wide range of sources to illustrate these trends and how the global patterns in terrorism and violence interact with Islam. It cannot overcome the lack of consistent and reliable data in many key areas, or the fact that many key factors do not lend themselves to summary quantification and trend analysis. It is also impossible to go into depth in analyzing the individual trends in Islam and extremism in a broad overview of global trends, or to highlight all of the limits in the quality and reliability of the data available.

The analysis does, however, make use of the same START database that the US State Department uses in drafting its annual country reports on terrorism. While there is no agreement between open source databases in terms of numbers, there does seem to be broad agreement as to the direction and intensity of most trends. Uncertain as the numbers may be, the vectors in these numbers do seem to reflect many areas of consensus.

It also draws on a wide range of other materials to reflect recent polling of Muslim opinion, data on the broader divisions that lead to violence and extremism in much of the Muslim world, and various official sources to show the trends in the current "wars" on terrorism, the degree to which partnerships between Muslim and non-Muslim states form the core of the effort to defeat extremism, and the extent to which the rise of extremism ensures that it may take several decades of active security partnerships to end the threat.

Global Patterns of Terrorism Are Dominated by Extremism in Largely Muslim States

The first section of the report makes it clear that the patterns of extremist violence are dominated by violence in largely Muslim states and by extremist movements that claim to represent Islamic values. It shows that the START database counts a total of 70,767 terrorist incidents between 2011 and the end of 2016. A total of 60,320 of these incidents—85% of the global total—occurred in largely Islamic states. A total of 51,321 of these incidents—73% of the global total—occurred in the Islamic states in the Middle East and North Africa or MENA region.

It is important to note, however, that only a relatively small portion of the incidents can be attributed to ISIS, even using the highest START estimate. More broadly, even if Afghanistan is added to the total for Iraq and Syria, the three major countries where the US and other outside states partner with Muslim governments accounted for 26,113 incidents—or only 37% of the global total. Moreover, even if one counts all of the MENA region and South Asia, key organized extremist groups like Al Qaida, Al Nusra, ISIS, and the Taliban accounted for 12,159 incidents or 17% of the total. Defeating today's key perpetrators is critical, but it in no way will defeat the longer term threat.

BUT, There Is No "Clash of Civilizations." The Vast Majority of Muslims Consistently Reject Extremism and Terrorism.

The second section of the report draws on a range of polls to put these statistics on incidents into perspective. There is no poll of opinion in every Muslim or Arab state, and many of the polls available—including the ones in this report—have serious flaws and limitations. Nevertheless, the polling data still seem good enough—and consistent enough—to show that the vast majority of Muslims do not support extremist violence, and that their primary concerns are jobs, the quality of governance, security, and the same practical values shared by non-Muslims.

Moreover, for all the talk of "foreign fighters," even the high estimates in the media represent a negligible portion of the total number of young men who might join in such movements. Arab youth do not support extremist violence. Moreover, the small portion that does in given countries in given polls is often reacting to a crisis in Israeli-Palestinian relations or some other major incident, and that limited support tends to drop sharply when it no longer is driven by the heat of the moment.

The Battle of Perceptions, and Popular Motives in the MENA Region and Islamic World

The third section supplements the second by showing that only 17% of Muslims saw religion as the key factor in recruiting fighters for ISIS, and that interpretations of Islam ranked seventh in a poll examining Arab views of ways to defeat extremism. At the same time, it warns that the rejection of extremism and terrorism does not and there was popular support for many US and other western foreign policies. Moreover, 77% of Arabs polled still felt that the Arab peoples were a single nation, rather than focused on the actions of their government and their own nation situation.

Casualties in the US and Europe Are All Too Real. But, It Is Muslims That Are the Overwhelming Victims of Extremist Attacks.

The fourth section of the report shows the trends in terms of death, injuries, and kidnappings/hostage taking. No one can condone or ignore the numbers killed in the US and Europe, but they are relatively tiny in actuarial terms. For example, there were 658 deaths in Europe and all of the Americas between January 1, 2015, and July 16, 2016. There were 28,031—or 43 times more deaths—in other regions—most of them consisting of largely Islamic countries. Almost all of the human impact of extremist attacks is Muslims killing or injuring fellow Muslims.

Seven of the ten countries with the most terrorist attacks in 2016 had vast Muslim majorities, and the death and injuries in the other three involve large numbers of Muslim deaths. A total of 83% of the attacks and 90% of the deaths occurred in solidly Islamic countries. The vast majority of suicide and vehicle attacks came from "Islamist" extremist groups that killed Muslims in largely Muslim countries.

If one looks at the five worst perpetrator movements in the world in 2016, four are "Islamist" extremist. A total of 88% of 2,916 attacks and 99% of 14,017 deaths that resulted from the top five perpetrators were caused by Islamic extremist groups.

Restrictions on Religion Attempt to Limit Extremism in Much of the Islamic World

The fifth section makes it clear that most governments in largely Muslim states are actively moving to suppress religious extremism in their country. State Department Country Reports on Terrorism and Treasury Department lists of designated groups and individuals funding terrorism show both major progress in largely Muslim states in fighting extremism and limiting the funding and support of extremist groups and that much more needs to be done.

At the same time, work by the Pew Trust highlights the fact that many largely Muslim states have placed growing limits on extremist preaching and religious activity. This necessarily interferes with freedom of religion and speech, and given states often exert excessive limits and control, but vague charges that such governments are failing to act do not reflect the real-world actions of many—if not most—governments in largely Muslim states.

Islamophobia Is Dangerous and Ignores Muslim Patriotism and Support for Their Country in Nations Outside the Muslim World

The sixth section provides a short case state in the dangers of Islamophobia. Polling data illustrate the degree to which American Muslims show consistent loyalty and support for the US. It also shows that the vast majority of terrorist attacks in the US did not involve Muslims, and that those attacks that did involve "Islamist" motives were generally by American-born Muslims or full citizens and not by recent immigrants.

The data also show that American Muslims have seen some slight rises in the violent impact of Islamophobia. The risks of becoming a US victim of Islamist violence have been tiny relative to other causes of death and violent death since 2011, but the size of anti-Muslim hate crimes has grown. Islamist violence still produces more deaths, but FBI reporting shows that anti-Muslim hate crimes produce higher levels of overall violence, rape, and serious injury.

Extremism Poses a Critical Threat to the Ability of Largely Islamic States to Meet the Needs of Their Rapidly Growing Populations

The data and trend charts in the seventh section provide a wide range of metrics showing the other pressures that divide largely Muslim states, and that can drive their populations towards extremism. Each can be a study in itself, but it is clear that many Muslims feel their governments are corrupt and that secular options fail to protect them and provide adequate future opportunities.

Population pressure and corruption are critical factors, as are ethnic and sectarian divisions and hyperurbanization. Youth lack jobs and opportunity in many states, and per capita incomes are sometimes critically low.

Islamic States Are Key Strategic Partners in the Fight Against Extremism, and the Rising Global Impact of Islam Makes These Partnerships Steadily More Critical

The eighth section of the report highlights two key factors in dealing with the threat of "Islamist" extremism. First, almost all of the states with large Muslim majorities have governments that already cooperate with the US in the struggle against extremism. These strategic partnerships are critical to containing the threat and limiting its impact outside the countries where it is now centered.

Second, the need for lasting strategic partnerships with Muslim states is reinforced by key demographic trends on a global basis. Work by the Pew Research Center estimates that the total number of Muslims will increase from 1.6 billion in 2010 to 2.76 billion in 2015—an increase of 73% or 1.16 billion people.

Dividing the world on a religious basis, or even seriously alienating a substantial portion of the world's Muslims could create all too real a clash between key elements of the global population and economy.

ISIS, Al Qaida and the Taliban Are Key Current Threats but Are Only One Small Part of a Far Broader Problem That Will Endure for Decades

The trend charts in this section reinforce the points made in the previous sections about the enduring threat that extremism and instability poses to the Islamic world and the state outside it.

When they are compared to the previous trend data on incidents and deaths, they show that Al Qaida, ISIS, the Taliban, and the other main targets of today's anti-terrorism and anti-extremist efforts are only a comparatively limited part of even current threats.

Even Total Victory in Syria and Iraq Could Only Have a Limited Impact: Most ISIS "Affiliates" Outside Iraq and Syria Are Not Closely Linked to the ISIS "Caliphates" and Will Survive ISIS Defeats in Iraq and Syria

It is also striking that ISIS's "affiliates" outside the current range of major military efforts—those only tenuously tied to ISIS central—have been responsible for more terrorist incidents than ISIS central has been in Syria and Iraq.

The Current Fighting in Syria and Iraq Is Unlikely to Bring Any Lasting Security and Stability

The data in this section of this report documents major progress in fighting ISIS and a major joint military effort between a US-led coalition and host country allies. It also, however, highlights the lack of any clear grand strategy to bring security and stability to Syria and Iraq. Defeating extremist organizations like Al Qaida, ISIS, and Al Nusra will be a critical step in limiting the threat, but even near total defeat of today's major perpetrators will leave major cadres and large numbers of fighters.

As yet, there are no indications that such defeats will be followed by recovery and reform efforts that will bring lasting security and stability to the divisions within Syria and Iraq shown in this section. Extremist groups will remain, governance and economic development will be weak and divided, ethnic and sectarian differences will be critical, and the outside role of powers like Iran, Russia, and Turkey will be deeply divisive.

Limited tactical victories are no substitute for a meaningful grand strategy that addresses the lasting outcome of such victories.

This Is Even More True of the Fighting in Afghanistan and Pakistan

The trend data in this section show that even tactical success is uncertain in Afghanistan and Pakistan.

Again, there is no clear indication of the capability to build on the defeat of the Taliban, Haqqani Network, and other extremist groups to bring lasting security and stability to either Afghanistan or Pakistan

Terrorism and Extremism in Yemen Have Become a Strategic "Black Hole"

The final section in the report provides a different kind of warning. It shows that the cost of failing to create effective strategic partnerships can be far greater and more destabilizing even if such partnerships only really address a limited part of a nation's tensions and divisions and focus almost exclusively on security.

Yemen is only one such case study. Libya, Somalia, the Sudans, and a number of Sub Saharan African countries already present similar challenges. The study referenced earlier in section seven, "Instability in the MENA Region, Afghanistan, Pakistan, and Key Conflict States: A Comparative Score Card," highlights the scale of these challenges and causes of current and future extremism.

Organizations to Contact

The editors have compiled the following list of organizations concerned with the issues debated in this book. The descriptions are derived from materials provided by the organizations. All have publications or information available for interested readers. This list was compiled on the date of publication of the present volume; the information provided here may change. Be aware that many organizations take several weeks or longer to respond to inquiries, so allow as much time as possible.

American Civil Liberties Union (ACLU)

125 Broad Street, 18th Floor
New York, NY 10004
phone: (212) 549-2500
website: www.aclu.org

The American Civil Liberties Union (ACLU) is a nonprofit organization founded in 1920 to defend and preserve individual rights and liberties guaranteed to everyone in the US. Two of its primary goals include protecting the rights of persecuted groups and protecting the freedom of expression and assembly, even if the message is disagreeable. It has defended controversial groups like the Ku Klux Klan, the Nation of Islam, and the National Socialist Party of America. The organization files legal cases in state and federal courts and advocates for legislative action.

Anti-Defamation League (ADL)

605 Third Avenue
New York, NY 10158
phone: (212) 885-7700
website: www.adl.org

The Anti-Defamation League (ADL) is an international Jewish non-governmental organization based in the US. It was founded in

1913 and works to oppose extremism and anti-Semitism. It tracks extremist groups on the far right and the far left and works with the FBI to share the information it gathers on these groups. It also campaigns for federal and state hate crime legislation, including anti-cyberhate laws.

Civil Rights Division of the Department of Justice

950 Pennsylvania Avenue NW
Washington, DC 20530
phone: (202) 353-1555
website: www.justice.gov/crt

The Civil Rights Division of the Department of Justice enforces federal statutes prohibiting discrimination based on race, color, sex, disability, religion, familial status, and national origin. It was created in 1957 by the enactment of the Civil Rights Act of 1957. It is led by the assistant attorney general of the United States and has been involved in many of the nation's pivotal civil rights battles.

Federal Bureau of Investigation (FBI)

935 Pennsylvania Avenue NW
Washington, DC 20535
phone: (202) 324-3000
website: www.fbi.gov

The Federal Bureau of Investigation (FBI) is the domestic intelligence and security service of the United States. Founded in 1908, it is the primary federal law enforcement agency of the country. It collects data on hate crimes as part of its civil rights program and investigates hundreds of cases every year. It works to detect and prevent incidents through law enforcement training, public outreach, partnerships with community groups, and supporting state, local, and tribal law enforcement groups in investigations.

First Amendment Coalition (FAC)
534 Fourth Street, Suite B
San Rafael, CA 94901
phone: (415) 460-5060
email: fac@firstamendmentcoalition.org
website: www.firstamendmentcoalition.org

The First Amendment Coalition (FAC) is an American nonprofit public interest organization that works to promote free speech, open and accountable governance, and public participation in public affairs. It provides legal supports to journalists and citizens to help protect their First Amendment rights. It also campaigns for First Amendment–friendly legislation and against bills that are perceived as working against free expression.

Foundation for Individual Rights in Education (FIRE)
510 Walnut Street, Suite 1250
Philadelphia, PA 19106
phone: (215) 717-3473
email: fire@thefire.org
website: www.thefire.org

The Foundation for Individual Rights in Education (FIRE) is a nonprofit organization that was founded in 1999 to protect free speech rights on US college campuses. It defends the right of campus organizations to freely host controversial speakers. They file legal cases on behalf of students and organizations whose free speech rights have been violated.

Muslims for Progressive Values (MPV)
162 N. Wilcox Avenue, Suite 702
Los Angeles, CA 90028
phone: (323) 696-2678
email: info@mpvusa.org
website: www.mpvusa.org

Muslims for Progressive Values (MPV) is a grassroots human rights organization with networks around the world. It was founded in 2007 to promote implementation of progressive values, such as human rights and gender equality, in the Muslim community. It aims to prevent human rights violations and hate crimes by Muslim extremists as well as Islamophobic hate crimes toward the Muslim community.

National Association for the Advancement of Colored People (NAACP)

4805 Mt. Hope Drive
Baltimore, MD 21215
phone: (410) 580-5777
website: www.naacp.org

The National Association for the Advancement of Colored People (NAACP) is a civil rights organization based in the United States. It was founded in 1909 by an interracial group that included W. E. B. Du Bois, Mary White Ovington, Moorfield Storey, and Ida B. Wells. Its mission is to secure political, educational, social, and economic equality for Black people in the US and to eliminate race-based discrimination and violence. It provides resources on hate crimes throughout the country as well as legislation to prevent them.

Not In Our Town (NIOT)

PO Box 70232
Oakland, CA 94612
phone: (510) 268-9675
email: info@niot.org
website: www.niot.org

Not In Our Town (NIOT) is a project of the Working Group, a California-based nonprofit media production company. It began in 1995 and uses documentary film, social media, and community organizing tools to stop hate, racism, and bullying. Its mission is to promote safe and inclusive communities. Though primarily operating within the US, it has expanded its anti-intolerance activities to countries around the world, including South Africa, Ireland, Ukraine, and Hungary.

Southern Poverty Law Center
400 Washington Avenue
Montgomery, AL 36104
phone: (334) 956-8200
website: www.splcenter.org

The Southern Poverty Law Center is an American nonprofit legal advocacy organization that focuses on civil rights and public interest law. Its "Hate Map" tracks 940 hate groups across the United States and its "Hatewatch" blog monitors hate group–related activities of the radical right. It publishes investigative reports on hate groups, trains law enforcement officers and shares key intelligence with them, and offers analysis to the public. Its "Teaching Tolerance" project provides free resources to educators to promote social justice and anti-bias.

Bibliography

Books

Edward Ball. *Life of a Klansman: A Family History in White Supremacy.* New York, NY: Farrar, Straus and Giroux, 2020.

Barry J. Balleck. *Hate Groups and Extremist Organizations in America: An Encyclopedia.* Santa Barbara, CA: ABC-CLIO, 2019.

Danielle Keats Citron. *Hate Crimes in Cyberspace.* Cambridge, MA: Harvard University Press, 2014.

Seyward Darby. *Sisters in Hate: American Women on the Front Lines of White Nationalism.* New York, NY: Little, Brown and Company, 2020.

Eamon Doyle, ed. *Antifa and the Radical Left* (Current Controversies). New York, NY: Greenhaven Publishing, 2019.

Eamon Doyle, ed. *Political Extremism in the United States* (Current Controversies). New York, NY: Greenhaven Publishing, 2018.

Phyllis B. Gerstenfeld. *Hate Crimes: Causes, Controls, and Controversies.* Thousand Oaks, CA: SAGE Publications, 2018.

Martin Gitlin, ed. *When Is Free Speech Hate Speech?* (At Issue). New York, NY: Greenhaven Publishing, 2017.

Deborah Levine. *When Hate Groups March Down Main Street.* Lanham, MD: Rowman & Littlefield, 2013.

David Neiwert. *Alt-America: The Rise of the Radical Right in the Age of Trump.* London, UK: Verso, 2017.

Christian Picciolini. *Breaking Hate: Confronting the New Culture of Extremism.* New York, NY: Hachette Books, 2020.

Michael R. Ronczkowski. *Terrorism and Organized Hate Crimes: Gathering, Analysis and Investigations.* Boca Raton, FL: CRC Press, 2018.

Pete Simi and Robert Futrell. *American Swastika: Inside the White Power Movement's Hidden Spaces of Hate* (Violence Prevention and Policy). Lanham, MD: Rowman & Littlefield, 2015.

Robert J. Sternberg, ed. *Hate: How It Originates, Develops, Manifests, and Spreads.* Washington, DC: American Psychological Association, 2020.

Nadine Strossen. *Hate: Why We Should Resist It with Free Speech, Not Censorship* (Inalienable Rights). New York, NY: Oxford University Press, 2020.

Stanislav Vysotsky. *American Antifa* (Routledge Studies in Fascism and the Far Right). Abingdon, UK: Routledge, 2020.

Jeremy Waldron. *The Harm in Hate Speech.* Cambridge, MA: Harvard University Press, 2012.

Periodicals and Internet Sources

Hannah Allam, "'We Were Blindsided': Families of Extremists Form Group to Fight Hate," NPR, December 12, 2019. https://www.npr.org/2019/12/12/787295283/we-were -blindsided-families-of-extremists-form-group-to-fight-hate.

Elizabeth Nolan Brown, "Steven Salaita and the Tyranny of 'Hate Speech,'" *Reason*, September 16, 2014. https://reason .com/2014/09/16/hate-speech-steve-salaita-and-civility/.

Shaila Dewan and Ali Winston, "In California, Home to Many Hate Groups, Officials Struggle to Find the Next Threat," *New York Times,* April 29, 2019. https://www.nytimes .com/2019/04/29/us/synagogue-shooting-fbi-warning.html.

Steven Greenhunt, "Yes, America Faces a Threat from White Nationalists. No, More Laws Won't Fix That," *Reason*, August 16, 2019. https://reason.com/2019/08/16/yes-america-faces-a-threat-from-white-nationalists/.

Colin Moynihan, "Far-Right Proud Boys Go on Trial, but Anti-Fascists Are Boycotting," *New York Times,* July 30, 2019. https://www.nytimes.com/2019/07/30/nyregion/proud-boys-nyc-trial.html.

Amber Phillips, "What Is Antifa?" *Washington Post*, June 15, 2020. https://www.washingtonpost.com/politics/2020/06/02/antifa-trump-terrorist-group/.

Nancy Rommelmann, "Portland Wants to Ban Hate Groups, Has No Idea How to Define 'Hate Group,'" *Reason*, February 12, 2019. https://reason.com/2019/02/12/portland-wants-to-ban-hate-groups-has-no/.

John Samples, "Why the Government Should Not Regulate Content Moderation of Social Media," Cato Institute, April 9, 2019. https://www.cato.org/publications/policy-analysis/why-government-should-not-regulate-content-moderation-social-media.

Liam Stack, "Over 1,000 Hate Groups Are Now Active in United States, Civil Rights Group Says," *New York Times*, February 20, 2019. https://www.nytimes.com/2019/02/20/us/hate-groups-rise.html.

Katy Steinmetz, "How the Internet Can Make Hate Seem Normal—And Why That's So Dangerous," *TIME*, October 31, 2018. https://time.com/5439713/online-hate-speech/.

Libby Watson, "Trump's Antifa Derangement Syndrome," *New Republic*, June 15, 2020. https://newrepublic.com/article/158182/trumps-antifa-derangement-syndrome.

Index